THERE IS MORE TO LIFE

By

David Walton

A 21st Century Heretic

Dedication

To my now ex-wife Steph, for putting up with me for over 30 years and all the wonderful things you taught me. To our children James, Ben and Sophie for being the beautiful people you are, you make me so happy.

Table of Contents

Part 1

Part 2

Part 3

Appendices

Part 1

The first 60 years

(In brief)

1 Introduction

How many times have you heard it said, or even said it yourself, "What's it all about? There has to be more to life than this?" At one time or another, most of us have said this or something similar. It seems however that there is little we can do about it. We look over the fence at pastures greener, thinking "If only…". However there is a lot more to life than we have been taught, a lot more to life than we appreciate, a lot we can do to improve how we experience it and that's what I intend to show you with this book.

In 2000, I won a huge contract. Well I say 'I won' but that's not entirely true as the other two consortium members and the team I headed would rightfully claim they played a big part. I was the British Telecom Bid Director bidding for the new accommodation building for GCHQ, (Government Communications HQ – it serves MI 5 and MI 6). The service contract was internally valued at over £1.5 billion.

There are not many contracts of that value available to bid. Winning it should have been the pinnacle of my career and on the CV it certainly was, however emotionally it meant nothing. I had no personal satisfaction, no high, and no glee; in fact it was the opposite. I sat in my office one Monday at a little after 8am and called all my internal stakeholders. I got voice mail after voice mail on which I left a simple message, "we've won." and hung up.

It should have been one of the best moments of my life but inside I felt very low and I said to myself, "There has to be more to life than this." Someone upstairs heard that plea as very soon I discovered there certainly is.

Within weeks I had what could be called an 'altered state of consciousness'. It was an experience not commonly accepted or considered normal. In fact many would explain it away as being a trick of the mind. However this was only the beginning and many more such experiences followed. Each one had an impact and little by little they changed my perceptions of what life is all about. So yes, there is a lot more to life than we in the Western world understand. I know it as I'm experiencing it and it's a lot more satisfying than working in the business environment, no matter how senior you are or how much money you may earn.

I have been gifted a first class ticket on a voyage of discovery that is by any standards absolutely awesome. I'm 16 years into it now and most has not been my doing, not my intention, not what I have been taught or read about. I'm a passenger, things just happen and some extraordinary things they have been. It has though taken me a long time to piece everything together and make sense of it all.

Over the past 16 years, I've felt the depths of deep despair. Separating from my wife had me questioning whether or not to just end it all. Yet within 20 minutes of being at my lowest and darkest point, I experienced the boundless joy of feeling like the most loved person in the universe. It is not surprising that this led to me questioning my own sanity. When things get shaken up to this extent anything can happen and things certainly began happening.

In 2012 my wife Steph and I separated and I left the UK to live in Dubai. Looking back, I was running away from everything and everyone I knew from the first 60 years of my life. I didn't realise it at the time but I had to shed 60 years of learnt behaviour if I was to discover who, or what, we human beings actually are; namely multi-dimensional energy beings with capabilities beyond our wildest imaginations.

I spent three years in Dubai discovering myself and discovering the authentic me. Today I'm a different person to the one I'd become living in England. I discovered soul regression that led to a past life regression course where so much was revealed and undone, so many of my beliefs explained and my behaviours understood. I travelled to Sri Lanka, Kenya and to Peru where I ultimately settled, well as there is so much change in my life I should say where I'm presently living.

What I now know is that there is so much more to life than we see on the surface. What our senses show us is only a very tiny percentage of what our life experience is really about. However, even this very tiny percentage doesn't provide an accurate image, it's filtered through the conditioning of Western society's accepted norms and as Quantum Science proves, it's an illusion.

I started having spiritual experiences when I was five years old however I suppressed them as these things are not spoken of, especially by a child. Following my plea in 2000 they started again and they have got increasing more spectacular even bizarre. I call them spiritual, as it's the closest term I have. Another and possibly more accurate description would be, I became aware of different dimensions of reality. Once we start considering spiritual experiences as experiences of other dimensions we see a more direct correlation with Quantum Science.

As Quantum Science tells us we are not solid, we are made up of pure energy. What spirituality adds is that our energy vibrates. What I have experienced is that different dimensions are just different vibrational ranges and I've been up the scale, high up that scale and deep down it though I'm not referring to despair. The vibrational range is just that, a range. There is no light or dark, that's just the interpretation that our senses provide.

I've been lifted to ride the energy waves of this third dimension to the very limits of its physical boundaries. It took me over 40 years to have the courage to allow my consciousness to expand to the very limits of the universe, to fill it, I have been one with it, completely. This may sound strange and contrary to many peoples understanding of what is possible, but I've done it, I have had the experience.

I've also experienced the lower vibrations through a direct connection with mother earth, who taught me the importance of remaining grounded, although that lesson had to be repeated many times. Through all the travel in the higher dimensions I wasn't as grounded as I needed to be.

I've seen three-dimensional creation at its very core, as sacred geometry describes, a beautiful toroid from which our reality is formed, I've seen it in operation, it is awesome in the true sense of the word.

I've stepped outside our concept of three-dimensional time, a very uncomfortable experience, very disorientating but I had to do this to understand that time is indeed an illusion.

We control what we experience and I explain how to control it. Although it is a simple process there are a few conditions and they sit deep within our unconscious mind. It's not just thinking about something, wishing for it or having the constant reminder of a vision board, there is more to it. Once we understand what we need to do, then we can start our journey and discover what life is really meant to be and that is considerably more than we experience.

My vibration has been lifted into higher dimensions to where we know deep within our consciousness the power we hold, ultimate power to create anything we desire. However with it comes the total lack of desire to create anything at all, as everything there is, absolutely everything, already lies within.

I've been shown the vibration of many higher dimensions that together with our known universe, our three-dimensional world, form creation itself. Creation just is, it is indescribable perfection. This may sound like a contradiction as the world we live in seems far from perfect, but that's because this world is the illusion that we, collectively, are creating.

I've felt divine love and utter bliss beyond imagination. Nirvana cannot be described in words, it is timeless bliss; being unconditionally loved by "All That Is".

To many these statements may all be a little difficult to accept. What I describe is contrary to what we are taught; contrary to traditional Western understanding, traditional science and religions. However recent developments in Quantum Science, Neuroscience and Cellular Microbiology have some very startling comparisons. There are an increasing number of scientists that are seeing the light.

I'm being taken on an amazing journey and when I look at all the things I've been shown and all the experiences I've had, I finally recognised they are all connected. What I have discovered has deep and profound implications for us all.

In this book I explain my life's journey, the events that led to the discoveries and how, when I was straying from my destined path, my guides intervened to get me back on track. And intervene they certainly did, it was the proverbial 2x4 to the back of the head.

My background would not make me a typical advocate of spirituality, I have had no spiritual teaching nor have I studied such things.

I've come though an engineering and commercial career. I've won and delivered large scale, high risk, multi-discipline programmes. I've worked at senior levels for major blue-chip companies, I've had the company Jaguar, a metallic gold XJ8, with champagne leather interior, it was very nice and it provided the external illusion of success. In the Western definition of success I probably was, but inside I certainly wasn't and the more I was shown, the more detached from the Western paradigm I became.

Buddhism was the obvious home for someone having the experiences I was having albeit they didn't originate through meditation. My experiences lead me to learn Reiki, NLP (Neuro Linguistic Programming) and hypnotherapy, then soul and past life regression. There has been more, all of which have played their part in increasing my appreciation of what I am and my life purpose.

When we move into higher states of consciousness we lose our learnt behaviour, our conditioning, how we've been programmed since birth to believe what we believe. Losing our conditioning is the most liberating experiencing one can have, it releases us from the tethers that hold us down.

Without our conditioned thinking mind to interfere with our observation we see this world from a totally different perspective; from a truer perspective. We begin to see reality and it is not what we presently perceive.

From this different perspective comes the appreciation of the nature of consciousness. Philosophers, sages and gurus throughout the ages understood consciousness but their wisdom has been lost as the West took the route of object-driven science and object-related proof. So much truth and wisdom has been ridiculed, dismissed as tricks of the mind.

I now understand how well developed ancient cultures actually were, indeed some not that ancient. The North and South American indigenous peoples knew so much more about the nature of creation and consciousness than their conquering masters. So much has been lost.

The West has lost its moral compass, lost its values that on paper may seem reasonable enough but in practice have caused a shift away from virtues and morality to one of a new God, that of money and the accumulation of wealth.

Everything is about money, however when we look at ourselves as human beings then it isn't money that makes us happy. This may seem a little controversial, as the lack of money can cause serious difficulties. It's hard to find happiness if you are being evicted. However it's not how we got into this position that this book is about, it's about how we can individually lift our vibration so we can appreciate the higher dimensions, where money and power over others isn't important.

We're conditioned from our earliest years to believe in the model of education, thinking that hard work brings progress measured by better jobs for the sake of more money. You need money as the marketers tell us that to be happy you need a bigger house, a better car, the latest gadget and designer jeans. If you are not climbing the ladder you're falling off it. What utter tosh, I've climbed the ladder and it doesn't bring happiness but we are told to believe it, after all there seems no alternative.

Well there is an alternative and you can choose it more easily than you would believe. Sound utopian and too good to be true? There are those with vested interests wishing to maintain the status quo who will tell you just that.

I ask you to decide for yourself but to make that decision you need to understand what the alternative is, and most importantly can it work for you, can it be practically implemented and if it can will it change your life for the better? Obviously I believe so.

A lot of what I write about I cannot prove, what is important however is how you feel when you are reading it. Do you feel intuitively it to be true? Your gut feelings are recognition created at a higher level. Believe in your gut feelings, your intuition, it will not mislead you.

Becoming aware of inner truth, rather than the truth we are told to believe in changes the baseline. It changes our understanding of life and our part in it as we all have a part to play, a soul purpose, a reason for being. However our soul purpose is drummed out of us by traditional educational and social systems.

We seldom act on intuition, we respond to our conditioned, educated, thinking, logical heads.

Imagine a huge iceberg yet only seeing the tip that is above the surface, this is where our thinking, educated mind resides. Whereas the might, the scale of consciousness is only appreciated when we look deeper.

Within the deeper elements of our consciousness lies the unconscious mind where we set the intent that we manifest in the three-dimensional world that we believe to be reality. Yes it is real enough but really it's an illusion. Once we see it for what it is, then we can begin to change it. Modification can be as easy as changing the content of a text message, but obviously before the message is sent. We need to be very clear about what we are sending right now because this is what we are creating.

Power of the unconscious mind

In 2007 I had a massive heart attack. It certainly was not my intent but I was able to put into practice something I'd recently learnt and this gave me opportunity to try it out, a true test.

Steph and I had been visiting Charlie and Janice, friends who had a villa in the south of Spain. We were all driving home together when the pains hit.

I was admitted to Burgos hospital that fortunately had a specialised heart unit and I now have a stent and even a DVD of the operation. It was six days before I was discharged and part of the discharge procedure was an echocardiogram. I was shown my pumping heart however a large part wasn't, 30 per cent in fact. It was explained to me I had 30 per cent scar tissue and I could see it. The doctor explained this was manageable as I had 70 per cent still functioning.

I asked why nearly a third of my heart wasn't working and the doctor drew me a sketch showing an electrical web over my heart and explained that part of the circuit had broken.

A few weeks earlier I'd completed an Advanced Hypnosis course with Dr Michelle Rhodes of Opal Training. Michelle spoke at length about Deepak Chopra's book *Quantum Healing* and I was taught the technique.

I began self-hypnosis, an hour a day reprogramming my unconscious mind as Michelle had taught. I set my intent, to repair the circuit around my heart, at the deep unconscious level.

On my return to England I went to Wythenshawe Hospital near Manchester and was under cardiac rehabilitation for six months. At the end of this period again a discharge procedure and this time some consternation. I knew something was odd when 20 minutes into the procedure I was asked to confirm my name, then my date of birth. I'd been through this twice already. Then the doctor said, "are you sure you had a heart attack?" "Yes" said I rather indignantly, to which he responded, "well there is no sign of it now, you have 100 per cent heart function, the Spanish obviously got it wrong."

I have a letter from Wythenshawe Hospital saying there was no damage to my heart and I have 100 per cent heart function. This is obviously good, however there was no investigation, no enquiry as to why my heart had miraculously healed itself.

At no time in Spain or in England did anyone ever suggest this could happen, there was no discussion ever about healing my heart. All I was told was how to maintain the condition with a concoction of prescription drugs. But why was there no investigation? I can appreciate doctors being busy but what is apparent is that there was no process to pick up on things that fall outside - or could challenge - conventional understanding or medical practice.

Challenging conventional medical practice is controversial as there are considerable vested interests in maintaining the status quo.

Dr Bruce Lipton is a cellular microbiologist whose research was into why, after a heart transplant, some hearts rejected. Lipton made a seemingly fantastic discovery; he discovered that it was the mind that controls the health of human cells. It is down to how we think. Lipton has two videos on YouTube.

<u>Bruce Lipton - The New Biology - Where Mind and Matter Meet 1 of 2</u> (1 hour)

<u>Bruce Lipton The New Biology Where Mind and Matter Meet 2 of 2</u> (1 ½ hours)

The first is a lesson on microbiology and the second is how he discovered the power of the mind over matter.

I know both Chopra and Lipton are right as my experience provides the evidence. It does though raise two issues, firstly and most importantly is the incredible power of the unconscious mind once we understand how to set our intent correctly and secondly why was there no investigation? If the data is not collected then it is easy to say there is no proof, write off my experience as anecdotal and blindly continue with the established tradition of doling out prescription drugs.

Some scientists have the evidence so why is it not part of our medical practice? Could it be that if people were taught to heal themselves, there'd be fewer prescription drugs sold?

To understand how our unconscious mind manifests intent we need to understand the rules it works by, and there are several. In brief we need to be aligned with our soul purpose whilst recognising and dispensing with the conditioning we have been subjected to since birth. Add to this an understanding of karma, vibration and connecting to the universe and we're on our way.

It may sound like a lot but once we understand it we can begin work and you'll be surprised how quickly you can address it.

> *What will result when you align your intent with your soul purpose?*

Throughout the book I reference doctors and scientists who have stepped out of their traditional boxes and seen the implications of recent discoveries, indeed many have made the discoveries themselves. I understand them as they resonate with my own experiences.

As with Lipton I reference several who have videos on YouTube and I provide the details, watching them will improve your understanding of the points we make. I summarise them to enable you to continue reading but if you can I strongly recommend that you watch them. In all there are over six hours of video. Some are only a few minutes, others over an hour, I provide the duration for each one and they are all listed in the appendices.

If you're using an e-reader that can utilise hyperlinks then just click on the highlighted title, otherwise I have used the same title as YouTube so if you're reading a hard copy book they can be found easily via a search on www.youtube.com.

You will discover there is considerable evidence from others that align with my experiences, however they're all individual and separate and it's not until they're all put together that we can see the big picture and what a picture it is.

So if there is so much evidence why is it not accepted as scientific proof? This is the first obstacle to understanding as many refuse to listen. I consider this to be important as throughout my life, when I've tried to explain the experiences I've had I've often been ridiculed and even called bonkers. "It's all tricks of the mind, there is no proof," detractors say.

If I'd had only one experience then it could have been difficult to maintain my position, the fact I've had so many and I've discovered others that explain similar experiences provide the evidence that it is nothing to do with tricks of the mind. However, what about the countless people who have had one-off experiences but suppressed them out of fear of ridicule?

One of the objectives of this book is to provide information and references that can be used to counter the objectors, to make it easier and more easily acceptable to discuss spiritual experiences.

I want to provide people who understand or who have had experiences with the evidence they need to support their case and to assure them that they are not alone. I wish to bring as many people as possible on the journey as this is how ultimately we will change society for the benefit of all mankind.

Some may say there is no proof to support what I say, it's anecdotal, this is the weapon used by skeptics. I set out to provide the evidence that we are energies well beyond the traditional scientific understanding. That we all have abilities well beyond our imaginations, that we are souls presently experiencing a life for a reason. Souls that chose to have many experiences of life, each one for a specific purpose.

Proof vs Evidence

Material science often says that there is 'no proof' to support what I'm writing about or in reincarnation or rebirth, however there is considerable evidence.

The key word here is 'evidence' and how it is applied and what is considered 'evidential'. Rebirth cannot be explained by traditional scientific method, however it is evidential as is explained in a wonderful book by Victor and Wendy Zammit, *A Lawyer Presents the Evidence for the Afterlife*.

Here is Victor and Wendy's explanation of what the High Court in a Western judicial system such as the UK House of Lords or the US Supreme Court, would consider technically admissible as evidential:

> *"Objective knowledge can be classified as scientific where the same results and the same 'cause – effect' connection can be demonstrated over time and space.*
>
> *"Science is regarded as 'objective' in that any person who follows the scientific formulas will get the same results."*

A defined process generates a set of results, when we do the same thing, somewhere else, with different people and get the same results then it's considered objective evidence, technically admissible in a Western High Court.

The Zammit's explain that there is overwhelming evidence for the afterlife, that could be termed the paranormal, but it is objectively evidential.

The afterlife is evidential. We need not be fearful of death, it is just the closing of one chapter enabling the opening of another. However this is the very small tip of this very large iceberg, as beneath the surface we find consciousness.

Consciousness is not physical. It cannot be measured and so is consequently ignored by traditional material science. However it is consciousness that survives the death of our physical bodies and consciousness that enters the embryo. It is consciousness that holds everything together and understanding this is the key to lifting ourselves into higher dimensions.

Rebirth has no scientific proof say the traditional scientists. Whereas there is formidable and overwhelming evidence, and if we examine it, look at the evidence there is only one possible conclusion, that there is rebirth. The point being is that the consciousness is not a result of who we are; consciousness is what we are and that's a lot more than we can imagine.

This is not what the West teaches or understands, it is counter to our philosophy and teaching.

To quote an old Irish joke, when an Irishman is asked how to get to a certain town, he replies, "if I was going there I'd not start from here". Well, starting from the Western paradigm isn't a good place to start discussing spirituality so the next two chapters unwind just a little of our Western conditioning.

In the rest of Part 1;

- I explain why I've used an astrologer, two psychics and a channelled entity called Zak. All of whom are referenced throughout the book. Fortunately I recorded the discussions, so I have been able to look back to discover how incredibly accurate they have been, the detail they provided astounding.

- I explain how to recognise what is our individual truth. I reference and expand on some brilliant work by Otto Scharmer of MIT.

- I describe the experience of being 'one with the universe', that resulted in spending 12 years attending the Buddhist Society of Manchester which led to the bliss of Nirvana. How these experiences were the start of developing my understanding of a multi-dimensional universe built on vibration.

- I explain how following guidance from above I created the conditions for my divorce and how desperately unhappy that made me. How from considering ending it all to bliss in 20 minutes made me question my own sanity.

However it was destined, it had to happen if I was to grow. Why I needed to leave everything I knew, 60 years of my life behind and move to Dubai.

Part 2 is about my three years in Dubai;

- How I began to rebuild myself, though a soul regression and many subsequent regressions on a past life regression (PLR) course. What retrieving a soul fragment felt like and dealing with a resulting 'Spiritual Emergency'.

- I describe my time in Kenya and being in the middle of a flash flood and what went through my mind facing imminent death. What young children in Nukuru's London slum taught me and what a profound lesson it was. Not all profound learning comes from gurus, some come from the most unexpected sources.

- I explain what standing outside time itself felt like and how disorientating and distressing it was.

- How mixing up e-mail addresses led me to a reading with a psychic that literally blew my mind and why I needed, and got, confirmation from another.

- I describe why moving back into the commercial world caused intervention from above and an accident that led to six hours of surgery and 12 days in hospital. Why again it was destined to happen and how this led to my discovery of the sacred plant Ayahuasca that ultimately created my move to Cusco's Sacred Valley in Peru.

Part 3 is about Peru;

- How arriving in Cusco, not speaking the language, having no plans and knowing one person who lived miles away, to within 2 months opening Munay Medicine, an

Ayahuasca and San Pedro (Wachuma) retreat in the Sacred Valley.

- I discuss my experiences with the sacred plants Ayahuasca and Wachuma and what amazing experiences they were. I found out why I had to come to Peru and particularly the Sacred Valley of Cusco, I'd been before several hundred years earlier.

- Despite the untruths of Western propaganda I've discovered how important these sacred plants are and how they brought me to understand amongst other things, creation itself.

- I discovered the ancient wisdom of Andean Cosmology, the knowledge of the Q'ero who were descendants of the Inca. It is so similar to Buddhism.

- What connecting to 'All That Is', the collective is like. How leaving it I was shown my life purpose.

- I explain a meditation taught me by Mother Ayahuasca on how to manifest our future.

I believe reading this book will enable you to understand there is so much more to life than we appreciate. Ultimately, regardless of how far you progress in this lifetime, I trust that you will see it for what it is and be able to enjoy it more.

2 Astrologers, Psychics and Channels

It is common for business executives to have a coach or mentor. I've been coached and have coached people. The coaches I've had helped me attain my business successes. When being faced with difficult decisions, feeling a little overwhelmed, or having doubts, it's good to discuss these issues with someone. It enables us to stand back and take a more objective view.

> It is difficult to smell the roses when you're
> up to your neck in shit.
>
> David Walton

Spiritual journeys can be very disorientating and confusing. It is more than fantastic to experience Nirvana but on the other side of the coin is a 'Spiritual Emergency'. This is when the inner changes come so thick and fast that the thinking head cannot keep up and dealing with everyday life can seem difficult. I've had two of these; they are not nice, at all.

My experiences have been going on for over 50 years and there is no manual. It is truly learning from experience and the experiences I've had have caused some confusion. Also it doesn't help when some questioned my sanity; I was doing enough of that myself.

If I had accepted others somewhat negative approach to my experiences, to have fallen inline with accepted norms, suppress and not live my truth then I'd not have made the progress I feel I have.

I did not find many open to the possibility that there could be something outside their understanding. I wonder just how many others have been in a similar position to me and concluded these others were right and just kept quiet.

Hence I was keen to meet anyone who could help me understand what on earth was going on. Buddhism was part of the answer but I also needed to find out why I was having these exceptional experiences.

Ki - An Astrologer that doesn't sugar the pill

In Jan 2012 my wife and I separated, I was in a mess and looking for help. A dear friend Pete suggested I speak with Ki an Astrologer. This was a challenge because I didn't accept astrology at all. From my vantage point I couldn't understand how a planet millions of miles away could influence my life. My view was misguided, I was certainly in a box with a belief and it was soon to be totally dismantled.

Ki did my Natal Chart, for those that understand Natal Charts there were a lot of red lines, which indicated a lot of opposing forces and inner conflicts. Within the first few minutes of our initial meeting I recognised myself in a manner I had not previously seen. Ki explained the issues I have been facing all my life and I started observing myself from a different perspective. It took a while to sink in but I was left with the question, just how much of life is predestined and how much is free will?

A couple of weeks later, with this question circling my mind, I went back to Ki for a forecast. He gave it to me straight. I was in for a rough ride for the next two years but I would handle it. I was on a lonely path across a desert but my destiny was an oasis where I would find happiness, love, wealth and great wisdom that I would teach. He said there was a lot of change coming, that after two years my wife and I would divorce and I'd be happy about it; it wouldn't bother me a bit. He also said I'd travel.

The thought of a two-year journey before things turned around was not telling me what I wanted to hear, neither was a divorce when I was still hoping for a reconciliation. I did not leave Ki in a

bubbly mood; in fact my 'self talk' told me it was all complete
rubbish.

Three years later what Ki said has proved very accurate. I'll not
be so quick to dismiss anything again. When disciplines like
astrology go back so far in our known history, is it surprising
there is something to it?

When we look at Quantum Physics and consider distant planets
as huge masses of dense energy, with energy fields projecting
across the solar system then perhaps it's a little easier to
comprehend how astrology may work. I don't pretend to have a
clue as to how astrology works but I cannot deny the accuracy of
Ki's reading.

Psychics

I've consulted with psychics all my life. I've had readings with
Madam whoever, sat on the pier of a seaside town with her
crystal ball and Tarot cards. Mostly just for fun, I never really
took too much notice but it was entertaining especially if you
could tie something together, which was more often than not a
challenge.

Then I met Nicola Pierson in Dubai, a psychic who came highly
recommended. Nicola read my palms and knew my past in great
detail; she identified my heart attack in 2007 and said I'd fully
recovered. She explained specific events that would unfold in the
very near future. She told me what would and wouldn't happen
and she was right, 100 per cent right.

She told me Christine Pearson, with whom I would do a soul
regression, would change my life, that Andy Tomlinson, who
would teach me past life regression, was part of that change. I'd
told Nicola who they were but at that stage had not met either.
She told me my planned trip to the Michael Newton Institute
(MNI) in San Francisco wouldn't happen and it didn't.

Then there's Melinda Adams in Brisbane, Australia. Oh Melinda! What Melinda told me was the most challenging and blew my mind but I knew, deep inside, at a fundamental intuitive level, it was truth. Melinda provided me with my big picture, like the lid of a jigsaw box and I saw where all the pieces, the individual pieces of my life, collected for nearly 60 years all fitted. I saw why my life was what it was and what I was to do. No vague generalisations, nothing but firm statements and they unfold later.

Channels

I also use a channel, Janet Treloar channels a spirit entity called Zak. I now consider Zak to be a friend having spoken with him on several occasions.

The first time I met Zak I was in a group of around a dozen people and I asked Janet if she would introduce him. I've watched YouTube videos of people like Darryl Anka who channels Bashar and the thought of speaking to a channelled entity myself was exciting.

We all had differing questions but one in common, how do we communicate better with our guides? At the end of the session Zak suggested we close our eyes and relax and they would communicate directly with us.

I was immediately filled with love, like a golden ball of pure love, it emanated from my heart and flowed through my body. I let out a deep sigh and as I did I heard others doing the same. We all felt the same thing and I immediately knew Zak is for real. Guides communicate through feeling, not words.

Zak's final words on that initial meeting were directly to me when he said, "and we shall be talking again soon". He was right of course. I spoke to him the following evening on a one to one basis for just over half an hour.

I recently asked Zak to describe his role for this book, a question he found highly amusing, replying that he's never been asked this before. He calls himself a "friend and overseer," someone who helps the guides of those in human form. He last incarnated as Zachariah in 1352 in Syria when he had a 'vacation life' as a shepherd. He is, he says, also in many other forms.

Zak also explained that he sees all possible outcomes. As we create thought, it is first recognised in our etheric field. It is, he says, "like a small bubble." As we give more attention to this bubble it builds in energy and grows until we manifest it in higher planes. Psychics see the etheric field and pick up on what appears to them as being the brightest bubble and most likely event to manifest.

I now understand this process a lot better albeit I don't consider it quite as easy as Zak's summary. We can all manifest our intent within constraints of our soul purpose, karma and the blockages of programming and conditioning that we create for ourselves. Once we understand how this works and follow that understanding then we can manifest what we desire.

Fortunately I recorded all my readings with Ki, Zak, Nicola, Christine and Melinda. I've listened to them a year or so after the readings and I'm still amazed at their accuracy. For me this all points towards my pre-destiny rather than free will.

3 Listening

Listening is an art and one of the most important factors in shaping who we are. When we are young, we accept everything we are told. This is where things begin to go wrong. Listening to others is where our conditioning begins and children are especially susceptible.

"Give me a child until he is seven and I will give you a man," is the Jesuit motto attributed to Saint Francis Xavier the co-founder of the Jesuit Order. The implication is that the best opportunity to indoctrinate a person in a lifetime of belief and devotion to religious dogma is when they are young.

This is one of the first things we need to recognise about where our beliefs come from and how we are conditioned to conform, not only to religious dogma but also to what society considers acceptable.

As adults we all think we listen, yet we all listen through a set of filters created through our upbringing, family, peers, education, culture, media, etc. This is how we are programmed, how we are conditioned, this is how our beliefs are formed. However much we may believe we're open-minded, it's only to a subjective extent. The ability to change our minds is truly liberating as it frees us from the need to be right. People who accept the possibility of being wrong are more open to new ideas and concepts.

Otto Scharmer, a senior lecturer at Massachusetts Institute of Technology's (MIT) Sloan School of Management, researched 1,400 companies on the US Fortune 500. He was looking for companies where the financial performance had been mediocre for many years. He wanted companies that had been performing significantly below their market average, then within a year to out-perform their market average by a factor of 3:1. He found 11 companies where there had been such significant and beneficial change, how?

The Board of Directors of the 11 companies Scharmer investigated had taken on a new director and this new director had changed how their boards communicated. No longer the fiefdoms of structure, now co-operation and collaboration based on feeling created change for the benefit of all. These companies reaped massive rewards. What was the difference? How they listened.

In his book, *Theory U, Leading from the Future as it Emerges (2009)*, Scharmer explains four levels of listening. *Theory U* provides a roadmap for leaders to create significant change by listening differently.

The diagram opposite is based on Scharmer's work. I have made some changes and added an additional listening level, Level 5.

We all like to think that we're open minded and few people would accept they live their lives in a Level 1 box, however it is the norm.

Listening is situational and controlled by a combination of different circumstances. We may pick on one situation where we identify ourselves as listening at Level 2 or 3 and use that to evidence our position, whereas the majority of the time we all prefer the comfort of our habits. It's how we are conditioned to behave and it's easy.

Listening behaviour

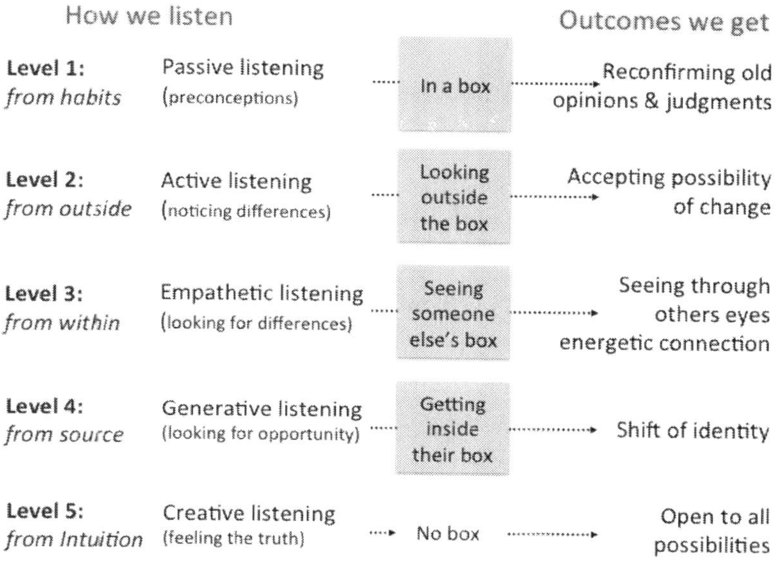

Like most people, I also like to think of myself as open-minded and yet I can still revert to Level 1. A few years ago our daughter Sophie rang from university, she was coming home for the weekend and was bringing her new boyfriend. Now this was totally new to us, she never introduced boyfriends, even denied they existed, so bringing one to meet her parents meant this was someone special. She added, "He's a cage fighter."

I was in that Level 1 box so fast. Despite knowing nothing about cage fighting I suddenly decided I knew everything I needed to know about cage fighters and I was certain they were not suitable my daughter. Preconceived ideas, I was hiding in a box. Well, Jamie was nothing like I expected. He's a warm, kindly and gentle soul who teaches Multiple Martial Arts (MMA) and held a 1st in Nutrition and Physical Education. I climbed out of that box pretty quickly.

Level 1 is being a 'close-minded skeptic'. It's the level where people cling firmly to beliefs regardless of the evidence to the contrary.

A statement like, "there is no such thing as UFOs and aliens" is an example of Level 1 behaviour, as it is impossible to prove otherwise.

In his *Disclosure on Bentwaters*, Lord Admiral Peter Hill-Norton, (Former Chairman of the NATO Military Committee – the most senior position in NATO), makes a very strong case for the existence of UFOs and in my view it's impossible to deny.

<u>The Lord Admiral on Bentwaters</u> (7 minutes)

An acceptance of the possibility that UFOs are alien craft is Level 2. You don't have to agree but you are open to the possibility.

At Level 2, we accept that we do not know something and so we will listen to others. It may be challenging but we will examine the evidence and there is a possibility we could change our minds.

Level 3 listening really understands what we're hearing regardless of our own prejudices. Again it may cause a change of mind, the important thing to recognise within self is that here you are not controlled by preconceived, conditioned beliefs.

In Level 4 we're looking for opportunity to 'add to'. We are shifting our identity and synchronising with another, using all our capacity to enhance their thinking. When we are in this level of listening, we co-create and the output is very powerful as it is greater than the sum of the parts. Consider when you last climbed into someone else's box, felt empathy for their position enabling you to co-create and what you achieved.

When we listen at Level 4 we are not just hearing the words, we are searching for the true intent, the feeling behind them. This I call vibrational communication and the vibration, or tonality of our words is where communication really lies.

Communication

Let's consider for a moment what we communicate when we speak and how it is listened to. Have you ever heard it said, "Well I told them and if they didn't listen then it's their problem?" Well is it?

The communication is what was communicated. If you send 100 bits of information and only 75 are received, what was communicated? The 100 sent or the 75 received? It is what the listener takes away that is the communication not what is said. However the most important thing is not what is said, it is how it is said, this is where the body of the communication lies.

Albert Mehrabian, currently Professor Emeritus of Psychology, UCLA, has become known by his publications on the relative importance of verbal and non-verbal communication.

A pioneer in the field, Mehrabian says that the meaning of a communication is conveyed by:

- The words communicate seven per cent of the communication,
- The tone of voice communicates 38 per cent of the communication and,
- The body language communicates 55 per cent of the communication.

Let's not get too hung up on the percentages, there are many that dispute them, however let's look simply at their priority. When we are communicating, the least important factor is the words we use. Next in significance is how we say them but the most important factor is our body language.

In Chapter 4, I describe our energy fields, and how we recognise the mental field, it provides a more detailed answer to the 55 per cent Mehrabian explains as 'body language'.

In Part 2 I describe what Mother Ayahuasca taught me about vibration. The tone of our expression, how we say something is considerably more important than the words we say. If we want to get the message across, it's our responsibility to ensure the listener understands what the message is, not just hang on to the words we use.

When we listen to others, we need to look behind the words. The meaning is how they are said and what you feel listening to them. This is Level 4 listening.

There is another level of listening not depicted in the diagram and I call this Level 0, this is negative listening. It's when people try to pick holes and destroy rather than find opportunities to add to and create. A typical example would be someone looking at 10 pieces of evidence and finding one that may have a flaw. Amplifying that flaw to discredit the proposition and enabling them to avoid examination of the remaining nine.

Level 0 is listening in fear. Hiding in a box with a rifle and the outcomes are negativity, it's the total opposite to a supportive creative approach. Level 0 does not accept the possibility that perceptions and beliefs may be wrong. Its avoiding 95 per cent of the evidence to concentrate on the five per cent that they can pick holes in. They will attempt to discredit anything that they don't understand. This is what some people do when they investigate the evidence of the afterlife, they focus on the five per cent that can be criticised and avoid the 95 per cent that supports the case.

Level 5 listening

The fifth level of listening is listening to oneself, it's intuitive, we are listening from inside to our gut feelings and shifting our learnt identity to align with our higher selves. When we listen to our intuition we are becoming authentic and recognising our truth. In this way our internal and external worlds become compatible. This compatibility, or congruence in self, is a vital step in lifting our vibration. This is something I return to many times, as this is where we will find our happiness.

Our intuition is usually non-verbal and purely feeling and comes from our spiritual guides. We get feelings like, 'I know I shouldn't be doing this...' Yet we do whatever it was anyway, as is the privilege of our free will. Often though the outcome is followed by, 'I knew I shouldn't have done that.' Logic, common sense, accepted norm it may have been but wrong it was.

When we listen at Level 5 we are being truly authentic. We are driven by a desire to help, support and above all create, we are following a higher direction our soul purpose.

Subtlety of feeling

A few years ago I passed a beggar on the street. As I walked past, offering nothing, I felt a subtle sinking feeling in pit of my stomach. So I stopped, turned back and gave the elderly man some change. He looked at me and as I felt his thanks, my heart lifted. There are some who believe that giving money to beggars is wrong, as they will spend it on drugs or alcohol, however few can argue that there are also those who are in genuine need.

Today, if I walk past a beggar and I do not get that sinking feeling, I continue walking. If I do get that feeling I recognise that this is someone in genuine need and I return to leave some change.

It's these intuitive gut feelings that today's material, object-driven science cannot measure so they are not considered important in explaining the world in which we live. They're often not even considered to be real. It is easy to see which level of listening these people use. They call their boxes "disciplines" and they have some pretty high sides.

> "Not everything that can be counted counts, and not everything that counts can be counted."
>
> Albert Einstein

Intuition can be confused with ego. Now I'm not knocking ego because without it we'd not be here. Ego creates the perception of separation, which is needed in our three-dimensional reality. However we do need to recognise when ego is talking, as that's what ego does, it talks. Beware the inner dialogue, our thinking talking minds can and do mislead.

Inner dialogue can sometimes be disturbing as something unsavoury or distasteful suddenly pops into our heads. Everyone gets these undesirable thoughts, however it doesn't mean they belong to us, they don't, unless of course we decide to claim them.

Consider standing in a river looking upstream at the water flowing towards and then past us. Consider this river as the river of our thoughts. You cannot see where they originate, as they flow towards us we recognise what they are. Here we make a decision, we can just let them flow past without examination or even examine them and then decide to put them back and let them flow past, gone. Or, we can hold on to them claim them, make them ours, it's our choice. The thinking mind is not what we are. We are the consciousness that decides how to respond to thought.

Here lies a fundamental observation as to what consciousness actually is. Traditional science considers consciousness to be a by-product of the awareness of our senses and that's it. However if that was the case, what is it that observes our thoughts and decides certain ones are unsavoury? What is the arbiter of thought?

The arbitrator is the observer it is the real you.

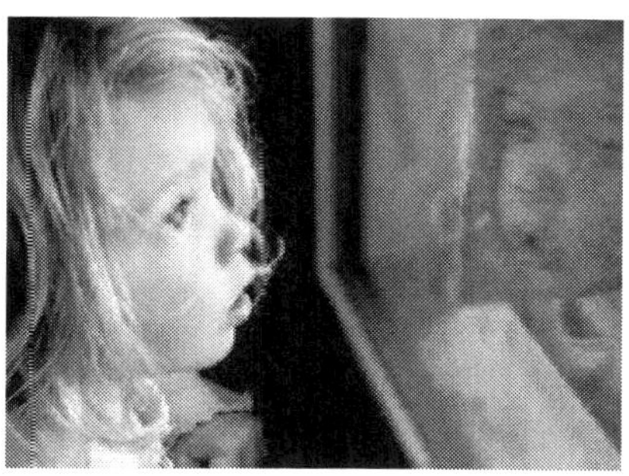

When you look in a mirror, what is looking at you?

You will recognise who you see, but what is doing the looking?

The real question is not who you are; it's what you are.

Sometimes when we look in a mirror we see someone not at our best and I don't mean how we've done our hair. Sometimes we just look older or more tired. Others times we look better and that may automatically bring a smile to our faces. What causes the difference and can we control it?

Thinking positively

The next time you notice you don't look as good as you'd like try this. Talk to yourself in the mirror. Better make sure the bathroom door is closed. Tell yourself how nice and kind you are, tell yourself how thoughtful and understanding you are, tell yourself how much you love you and how deserving of love you are. Mean it, do it with conviction. Remind yourself of all the kindness you have shown to others. Think of those you love and bring love into your heart. Notice the rye smile that has appeared and how differently you now perceive your reflection.

When we are positive about ourselves, our unconscious responds accordingly and we feel better. Our unconscious is filled with our conditioning it is what we manifest, our higher self is direction we recognise through feeling. When walking past a beggar, it is our higher self that recognises real need and it is higher self that provides the sinking feeling enabling us to change our minds and return to leave some money.

It is the higher self, our soul that comes back and that lives once more through a different body and a different set of eyes. It's not the person you see in the mirror but the one that is doing the observing. The person you see in the mirror is the one living the experience of this life with all the baggage, learning objectives and karma that comes with the package.

Higher self has ultimate patience is doing its best to help guide us through this complex maze to the discovery of our purpose set out for this lifetime. Sadly we don't always listen to this inner wisdom as many of us have lost the ability to feel, to recognise our soul, our intuition. We've been taught to think and reason and we call this free will. In reality, this is the cause of so many problems in the world today.

When we recognise our true motivation is love, compassion and forgiveness, then it's truly from source, higher self our soul. If our motivations are laced with retribution and revenge, one-upmanship or negativity then it's ego-driven, inner dialogue, free will, baggage.

Some people have totally switched off their intuitive senses and the consequence is an ego-driven need to control, so we have aggression, conflict and wars.

How can we reconnect with our higher, intuitive selves? In Chapter 7 I describe changes in people caused through Near Death Experiences (NDEs), these people re-associate with the identity of their higher self, their souls and the actual death is that of their conditioning, the conditioning that creates the barriers between who we perceive ourselves to be and what we really are. NDEs create a big shift to help us recognise what we are and in so doing we can start our real journey into spiritual growth by following our soul purpose.

However we don't have to go through an NDE, you can just re-learn or re-member Level 5 listening and reconnect with the real, true and authentic you.

When we tune into our intuition and recognise it is driven by love and act on it, then we become more internally congruent, which lifts our vibration. Things will then begin to run smoothly, although initially it may seem the opposite. Acting on your feelings can be challenging but if we are to lift ourselves into a higher vibration this is what we need to do.

I like to say that it's the difference in trying to push water uphill as opposed to downhill. Following our feelings is watching water run downhill, it takes no effort and we become the observer of life and surrender to the direction, without expectation. We go with the flow.

When we go with the flow, we're following our soul purpose. This brings with it enthusiasm, motivation and creativity. Too often we follow what we believe to be the route of minimal effort to make the maximum return. We follow the direction of our conditioning and do things within a predefined set of rules that tell us to do what we're told we're good at.

These rules are first learned in school. They apply to the thinking mind and a judgement on what you need to do to get a job. On revealing our dreams to a parent or teacher, how many of us have been told, "Oh you don't want to do that, there's no money in doing that."

Making money has become the objective and education follows that path, despite the evidence that educational systems serve less than 50 per cent of pupils.

Sir Ken Robinson gives a wonderfully colourful, entertaining and humorous TED presentation on how schools restrict personal growth, if you haven't yet seen it I recommend you do.

<u>Do Schools Kill Creativity? | Sir Ken Robinson | TED Talks</u> (20 minutes)

Robinson was a Professor of Education so he speaks with authority however more importantly he speaks from the heart. He explains how our educational structures were created and how these structures favour academia and by so doing restrict individual personal development and growth.

Another fascinating and more detailed explanation given by Robinson can be seen on this RSA Animate video;

<u>Changing Education Paradigms</u> (11 minutes)

This video is the most watched TED Talk and provides considerably more information. Robinson questions medical fashion, how it is used to medicate children that do not fall within a standard educational model. He explains the educational system is designed around standardisation and hence does not support the individual, and how it restricts creativity, something I'll come back to. Highly informative, he questions many accepted norms.

The education system provides training in the disciplines most needed in commerce. It doesn't address our individual needs, well unless you have been very lucky. I was one of the unlucky ones as I was a relative failure through the educational system gaining only two GCSEs but this was a blessing in disguise.

> "Sir Paul McCartney went through his entire education without anyone noticing he had any musical talent at all.
>
> 'The Element – Finding your Passion'
> Sir Ken Robinson

It is easy to see why I believe that the higher up the spectrum of conventional education you go, the less likely you are to accept the possibility that you could be wrong and end up in a Level 1 box.

Our education systems and religious teaching have created Western societies accepted norms that form the general rules we follow. Reincarnation or rebirth is rarely spoken about in the West and hence it becomes 'unaccepted' by the majority of people. This is despite the evidence and the number of religions that believe in it.

Rebirth challenges those with strong religious and particularly Christian beliefs. However Rebirth had been a major tenant of Christianity only removed in the 6th century.

In his book, *"The Case for Reincarnation"*, Joe Fisher explains that Reincarnation has been an accepted principle of Christianity and was accepted by Jesus Christ. Reincarnation was part of early Christian teaching until the conquest of Christianity by the

Roman Emperor Constantine. Constantine removed reincarnation from Christian philosophy; he believed it undermined his authority.

Resolving Personal Conflicts

Once we recognise these different levels of listening within ourselves we will observe others and then there is a potential to make judgements, which is something we need to avoid. Observation is one thing, judging someone is something else.

Judge Softly – First Verse

Pray, don't find fault with the man that limps,
Or stumbles along the road.
Unless you have worn the moccasins he wears,
Or stumbled beneath the same load.

Mary T. Lathrad
1895

However there is another side to this particular coin. You may decide that certain friendships do not serve you in the manner you may desire and that is a consequence but one that will serve you better in the long term.

We don't have this luxury at work, where there are rules, regulations, processes, procedures and a hierarchy of management structure. We fit in or we're got out. Being out of the corporate structure has enabled me to release stresses that lowered my vibration. Now I'm not suggesting leave your job just to recognise the potential for inner conflicts.

It is my belief that it is value conflicts that leads people like Chelsea (Bradley) Manning and Edward Snowdon to break with convention and imposed rules, to do what they felt was right. I believe they were driven by their intuition.

Conflicts are not always down to values or ethics; we can have disagreements with people that hold the same values.

Have you fallen out with someone, had a disagreement about something now seemingly trivial but since that moment have not spoken? It may be a friend or relative but you wish it had never happened? If so, recall that time now and think from what level you were listening. Never mind them, this is you, were you at Level 4? Well probably not, more likely Level 1.

Think how you would feel if that person rang you right now and said, "for my part in our fallout I am truly sorry". How would you feel and how would you respond? Think about it, if it'd make you feel good then why not initiate the call yourself?

If you don't get the response you'd have liked then there is nothing more for you to do, you have released your part of it and if they chose to hold on to bad feeling then it's their choice, their free will. Chances are though if there was real friendship within the relationship it will re-ignite and you will both benefit.

The point here is that if you want to move up the vibration ladder to see life differently you need to be aligned with inner self and address, not supress, any conflicts.

Holding onto bad feelings lowers your vibration it's baggage, it serves no purpose. Blaming others is not the answer, the only one responsible is you. Get rid of it as soon as possible, make that call, go and see that person, make it right. You will know you've done the right thing due to the feelings you get, letting go of the baggage brings rewards.

4 The Universe Lies Within

Think of this.

A wife is preparing food in the kitchen. She has her back to the door her husband is just walking through. Yet before a word is said, without the facial expression to guide him, he immediately knows he's in trouble.

How many men have been there? Women know they can create an atmosphere just by adopting a certain state of mind it's a choice. It works both ways round as men can do the same.

What creates this atmosphere? There are countless other examples like when someone walks into a room with a black cloud over their head, well not literally, but we feel it. Often we read physiology but not always. So what's happening when there is nothing said and no physiology to interpret?

When you meet someone new, it may be a friend of a friend, you decide very early on if you like that person. You get either good or bad vibes. Sometimes very strongly, other times it's more subtle.

For those that interview people, they often make up their minds before the interviewee has even sat down. This may sound unfair but when I joined a VT Group a few years ago I was interviewed by the Commercial Director and I later asked him at what point he'd made up his mind. He said, "when you walked through the door".

Have you ever been thinking about someone and suddenly the phone rings and it's them? Dr Rupert Sheldrake has, through considerable research he has developed a hypothesis he calls 'Morphic Fields' and 'Morphic Resonance' that addresses this and other similar and unexplained phenomenon. Morphic fields provide a very convincing argument about how fish shoal and birds flock, how dogs know when their owners are on their way home and how cats know to hide when they are due to be taken to the vets. His book *'The Science Delusion'* is well worth reading.

If you think about it you will have your own examples or similar experiences. We often call this a sixth sense and yes that's exactly what it is, so we accept it but ask a traditional neuroscientist to explain it, they can do very well with the five senses, but six is a sense too far.

Apart from Sheldrake's work I know of no other scientific explanation, but we know it happens, we've all experienced something similar, and too many times for it to be coincidental. Traditional science has been very clever in what it's achieved however there are some gaping holes in its and our understanding.

Your own experience tells you there is more to what is going on than we understand and can scientifically explain, or go through an empirical process to replicate and 'prove'. This doesn't mean it isn't happening every minute of every day. All it means is, we haven't yet got the scientific tools to understand and measure what is happening, or have we?

Energy Fields

I'm very familiar with energy fields, auras and our chakras. I've formally trained as a Usui Reiki Master Trainer and learnt other energy healing techniques. I favour a Q'ero method. The Q'ero are a small community of farmers, weavers and medicine people who live at the highest altitudes of the Andean mountains in Peru. They sought refuge in these mountains when the Spanish invaded in the 1500s.

The Q'ero do not see themselves as separate beings as we do in the West. They believe in the collective spirit, they know that we're all one with each other as well as one with nature and with God. They do not even have a word in their language for the concept of 'I'.

When I do energy healing I combine Reiki and the Q'ero methods as there are some strong similarities. Energy healing goes back centuries, it crosses many continents and cultures with many commonalities.

When I teach energy healing I always start with a wonderful video by Dr Sue Morter in which she does a brilliant job of explaining energy fields.

TEDxNASA - Dr. Sue Morter (18 minutes)

I started seeing auras in the last few years. I've been able to sense the fields through feeling since my Reiki 1 course in 2003. As Morter explains, there are three main fields that form our aura.

The first is the etheric field it is about 5mm deep. The etheric field is the blueprint for constructing the aspects of the physical body. It merges with the embryo during pregnancy and carries physical features such as birthmarks, wounds or injuries. It is this field I used in repairing my heart.

This is a very easy field to sense through feeling and one of the first demonstrations I do when teaching energy healing.

The second energetic layer is the Astral field, also called the emotional body, which carries our emotional baggage and typically expands half a meter around the body. This field can be seen in different colours. I have seen it as a neon yellowish gold, bluish and shades of green. I cannot always see it, I have to be in the right state of mind and I cannot always control my state as much as I'd like.

Third is the mental field. This expands several metres outside the body. It's the mental field that reflects our thoughts. It is this field that the hapless man I mentioned sensed when he walked into the kitchen and felt he was in trouble.

Earlier I mentioned Albert Mehrabian's work on non-verbal communication where he states that 55 per cent of communication comes from physiology. I'd say it comes through the mental field. We become aware of the feeling that sets the scene for the forthcoming communication.

Morter also describes the Universal field, which is beyond the mental field. I discovered this field in 2000 after 40 years of recurring so-called 'nightmares'. Since the age of five I'd sensed a boulder at the end of my bed that threatened to crush me.

My boulder provides a quantum leap

Although I didn't realise it at the time, my first experience of an altered state of consciousness or expanded awareness can be explained by the movement of my awareness through the etheric, astral and mental fields leading to ultimately connect with the outer universal field that Morter describes.

At the age of five though, I didn't know this. All I knew was that there was something at the end of the bed. It was invisible but I felt it. It was about a metre in diameter and impenetrably hard, I called it a boulder and I felt it would crush me. I was very frightened and screamed.

My mum and dad came in and tried to calm me. I insisted there was a boulder at the end of the bed and it was going to crush me.

My parents called it a nightmare and told me there was nothing there and nothing to be frightened of, that it was all in my mind. They tried everything to settle me down. I couldn't convince them there was a boulder at the end of the bed and it was going to crush me. I couldn't explain it, I knew it couldn't be seen, that they couldn't see it, that nobody could see it, but it was there, I felt it, I knew it. But who would believe a five year old?

My boulder visited perhaps five or six times a year, I leant to suffer in silence. It was pointless calling my parents because they didn't believe me, always insisting it was a nightmare, always insisting there was nothing there and nothing to be frightened of even though I was clearly absolutely terrified.

I was visited for over 40 years and it always came first thing in the morning. I always reacted the same way, I'd feel a tingling down my spine, a little like a shiver, it would start at the top of my neck, run across my shoulders then down to the small of my back. I'd feel cold on the inside. The feeling would remain as long as the boulder did, which I guess was a minute or so. Then it would go just as fast as it had arrived. I always felt the same, as if I'd be overpowered and crushed by it.

As the years passed, I became accustomed to these visits so the intensity of the fear diminished as nothing ever happened but I still had very the same physical reaction. I felt I'd be overpowered and I always found it very unsettling. I started to question my own sanity. Psychologists called it a panic attack, it wasn't but I had no idea what it was. It was real, intense, strong, hard, round and invisible in everything but feeling.

Then I met a lovely psychologist Glenda Findlow. Glenda introduced me to the wonderful world of hypnosis and we began a search for the boulder. We found nothing but I found the experience of being in a hypnotic trance exquisite. Glenda suggested I read *Living Magically* a book on meta-physics by Gill Edwards, so I did. *Living Magically* seemed obvious, though it turned everything I'd previously understood upside down.

Glenda was due to go on a weekend retreat with Gill but unfortunately for her she couldn't attend. Interestingly when she booked the event she said she had a suspicion she wouldn't be able to go and she was right. Glenda offered me her place and needless to say I accepted. I spent a fascinating weekend with Gill near her home in the beautiful Rydal, a few miles from

Ambleside in the English Lake District. Rydal is an absolutely beautiful place I have been back many times.

Gill listened to my description of my boulder and how it affected me, how long I'd been experiencing it and my fear of being crushed. She probed into my feelings and how I managed them. Finally she suggested that I call on my guides for support and that the next time it arrived, I should invite it in rather than reject it.

This was a terrifying thought. I'd been living with this fear for over 40 years. Gill's suggestion that all this time I'd been doing the wrong thing was horrifying. I didn't imagine I would be able to do as she advised but it was the first time I had an option.

A few days later I was back in Cheltenham with the bid team waiting for the results of months of stressful work bidding for GCHQ. In Cheltenham, my boulder was the very last thing on my mind. However, it was not long before it made it's last very dramatic appearance.

It was around 6.30am on a Saturday morning, a couple of weeks after I'd made my plea that 'there must be more to life', when the boulder was back, bigger and stronger than ever. I'd just been to the bathroom and got back into bed.

My spine tingled and I broke out in the cold sweat, my blood ran cold. The boulder was at the end of the bed, this time slightly to the left. Again I felt I'd be crushed and as I thought about what Gill had said I realised I couldn't summon the courage and that made me slightly unsettled.

This time it didn't go, it stayed a lot longer than it ever had before, as if it was challenging me. I felt that I was left with little option so finally I called for my guides, my late father and all the deceased relatives I could recall. I asked for their protection and support. I took a deep breath and just as I was about to accept it, in that instant, in that very moment, the boulder entered me. It entered right into the middle of my chest, and so incredibly fast, I was possessed by it but I wasn't crushed, quite the opposite.

The next few moments were awesome, I felt myself expand, my whole essence, my whole being expanded, I got bigger and bigger. I was the size of the house, as big as the country. I was bigger than the planet and I was still expanding. I felt I could hold the planet in my palm of my hand and I grew even more, the earth became no more than a speck of dust at the end of my finger. Then I seemed to accelerate in every direction simultaneously. I was travelling everywhere, all at the same time and so incredibly fast. The only way I can describe the feeling is that I became the universe. The scale was immense, I was everywhere in the universe simultaneously. Everywhere. I was the universe; I totally enveloped it.

"Wow what a trip," I thought, and in that very instant I was back, normal size, lying in bed, wondering what on earth had just happened and being somewhat disappointed the journey had come to such an abrupt end. It had probably lasted no more than 20 - 30 seconds, but I really have no idea.

It is difficult to describe something that sounds so different to accepted reality. The feeling of being such an immense size and travelling in all directions at the same time is as close as I can get to describe something so profound and astonishing.

Since then my boulder has not been back. I now understand that it couldn't return because I still contain it. My boulder was in fact another part of me and I had to invite it in and when I did, it brought a homecoming present.

No one could help me understand my boulder. No one could explain it and the general consensus was I maybe just a little bonkers. It did though lead me to Buddhism.

I explained my experience to Russell Williams at the Buddhist Society of Manchester. He and about half a dozen others listened and smiled. Not a smile at me, as I was more accustomed to, but smiles with me, as they knew.

After I'd finished the explanation, Russell asked gently, "Would you like to do it again?" Yes was my obvious answer and he taught me a meditation practice.

I have never since reached the same immense scale, I've once managed the size of the Earth but most commonly it's just a few metres. I teach this practice, as I believe it is important to experience expanded awareness; to know that consciousness is not limited to the constraints of the physical body.

Don't expect though that a few lessons on meditation you can become "one with the universe". As Sue Morter explains in her TED talk, we create our own blockages or interferences in our energy field through thoughts of frustration, fear, anger and hate.

Like a brick wall that blocks the sunshine from reaching our physical bodies, these interferences can limit the experience of expansion of awareness. At a rough guess I'd say around half the people I teach do experience an expansion of their awareness. I believe for those who are not able to experience the expansion it comes down to these blockages. Happily, says Morter, they can be dissolved with thoughts and feelings of love, forgiveness, gratitude and acceptance. These emotions we generate from the heart space are considerably more powerful than thoughts born out of fear.

Why was I given a free pass to such an experience? I can only surmise it was an introduction. Its purpose was to show me my destiny. Unknowingly I made it wait until I could see the futility of the path I was following when I said, "there has to be more to life than this". It had to wait until Gill Edwards gave me the insight, until I opened my mind and left the box I'd been occupying for 40 years, then as soon as I'd made the decision it knew.

Meeting Gill Edwards was a significant step in my spiritual development. Glenda led me there and I sincerely thank them both. From this point a lot began to change, on reflection more changed than I could ever have realised. Imagine setting off in one direction, then just changing course by just five or 10 degrees. Twelve years later that small change created a significant shift.

A few months after our separation in 2012, I asked Steph the standard question, "Where did it all go wrong?" She asked for a few days to think about when her feelings for me changed. She came back a couple of days later and said, "It was after GCHQ, nothing was the same after that."

From that point on I was on an immense voyage of discovery, indeed I still am.

5 Vibration and Dimensions

Vibration

Within the quantum world there is string theory. These strings are so very small that it's difficult for the human mind to comprehend. The average size of such a string is called the Planck length, which is about 10^{-33} centimetres. Put another way, 33 zeros behind the decimal point, so small we can hardly wrap our heads around it. These strings vibrate at different frequencies to form the fundamental particles that create the atoms that form molecules that combine into cells from which we are all made.

Everything in the universe is energy vibrating and we do the same but not at the sub-atomic level, it's the vibration of our unconscious minds. When we talk about our vibration we are talking about the vibrational rate that is held down by what else is held within our unconscious. The unconscious is what we access in hypnosis it holds everything we have ever experienced, it is here our conditioning is held. Our conditioning is the barrier to connection with our higher self, this holds down our vibration.

The higher self has a very high vibrational rate, much higher than our unconscious. When we lift our vibration to match our higher self we have become truly congruent and able to transcend the physical.

We are all at different positions on the vibrational ladder. I imagine these to be like octaves on a musical scale. I believe there are three octaves and we all live within the range of our octave and we can move up to a higher one by listening to our intuition and becoming more congruent with higher self.

A person experiencing life in a higher octave finds more happiness than a person living in a lower one. Their experience of life is different. They may see the same image, the same flower or tree but perceive them differently.

I've shifted octaves going up the vibrational ladder to have some wonderful experiences. Sadly living in the Western world I've shifted down again to what some may call the 'real' world, other than I know it isn't.

The higher we vibrate, the greater our awareness and this is where we find greater understanding and acceptance. This is where love for all things becomes truly integral, as this is what we are, love.

Going back to the levels of listening, Level 1 is a low vibration whereas Level 4 is higher as obviously is Level 5. People can lift their vibrational rate by deciding how to listen; it's a conscious choice. Losing judgement is a conscious choice; it's how we chose to listen that controls how we experience life. It really is that easy.

We are all multi-dimensional beings, all capable of traversing the dimensions. We are all here for a purpose and what is holding us back is our baggage, beliefs, pre-conception, judgement, etc. When we recognise this and act on it we shift up, everyone can do this.

Higher vibration brings greater intelligence that leads to wisdom and it is important to distinguish the difference between cleverness, and my definition of intelligence and wisdom. People can be extremely clever as measured by our academic educational systems, however that does not mean they are intelligent or wise. Many may have been considered to have 'failed' the educational measurement systems and yet are very intelligent indeed.

As an example, it is very clever for a few to manipulate the financial markets for their own benefit but the detriment of many, however it is not intelligent or wise. Similarly it is very clever to design and build nuclear weapons but again it is not intelligent. The West is clever, it understands cleverness but it is not intelligent and doesn't understand wisdom. Just look at the mess we're presently in.

The universe is consciousness, a higher level of vibration, however Western culture has gone down the Newtonian science route to consider everything as objects. The truth is that objects, humanity, and everything in existence is purely energy vibrating. Once we understand this, really understand it, then the ramifications fundamentally change our view of the world and our purpose for being here.

Higher dimensions are just a higher vibration. The experience of being 'one with the universe' is outside the understanding of our Western world. My vibrational rate went higher than Western culture can understand. I see it as entering the fourth energy field, the universal field.

I still perceived the universe as material, vast as it may be I was just so much bigger. So I believe it was still a third dimensional experience but from a different perspective. Or maybe I entered a higher dimension, I do not know.

Moving above our 3D universe to understand higher dimensions is difficult. Mathematicians and physicists talk about a multi-dimensional universe and I recall one who said that mathematically there could be 11 and no more. We cannot begin to comprehend what an 11 dimensional universe may be.

The complexity we face in trying to understand and explain the experience of higher dimensions is nicely described in an entertaining video featuring Dr Quantum.

<u>Dr Quantum - Flatland</u> (5 minutes)

Two-dimensional beings cannot understand living in a three dimensional world just as three-dimensional beings cannot understand five dimensions, etc. We can begin to grasp the concept through mathematics but that's theory and not the experience of it.

Just to clarify, time is often referred to as the fourth dimension so stepping up one takes us from our third dimensional world into the fifth dimension, 5D.

I have no way of knowing if being 'one with the universe' was a 3D or 5D experience or indeed something higher. There was no sign saying, "Welcome to the Fifth." There was no passport control and I didn't bring back any souvenirs. It's difficult to imagine a 5D fridge magnet, as there's no need for fridges where I went or any other material object.

The Fifth Dimension

I've read others interpretations of the 5D and they do not align with mine, so this is my explanation. 5D is still a physically manifest state albeit a totally different physical experience of that of the 3D world we perceive.

In 2015, I had an experience that according to ancient Andean Cosmology is 5D. I have accepted the interpretation I was given as it accurately described what I experienced. I describe the event in Chapter 17, it was as if I touched the hand of God.

In the 5D, we see and feel things differently. Rather than using our physical senses, our consciousness enters the etheric energy field. The etheric field is not restricted by our unconscious or the interpretation of the world through our five physical sense organs, which have filters and physical limits. Whereas our etheric field doesn't have physical limits.

Sensing through our etheric bodies is a different experience. It provides more saturated colours and more contrast with much greater range, definition and clarity.

As we're not using our thinking heads, the ego closes down so our unconscious mind doesn't interfere and we have greater ability to sense the subtlety of our feelings. We are given greater freedom and the natural state of love prevails throughout our being. Everything looks more beautiful and we feel more love. It is a higher vibrational rate, a totally different state of being.

When we've moved our consciousness into the etheric field we've made the first step and continuing through to the, emotional and mental fields is just continuing up the vibration ladder to the universal field where I was 'one with the universe'. As the Andean Cosmology interpretation of 5D aligns with one of my experiences I am forced to conclude that being 'one with universe' is indeed higher than the 5D, so for now I'd say it's the sixth dimension.

Behavioural Kinesiology

This is a complex topic with much research. There are many doctors who support and practice kinesiology, and there are of course detractors. I have had kinesiology applied to me and I've done it on others, in my experience it works very convincingly.

In the most simple of explanations, if you extend an arm to the side so it is horizontal and another person pushes down on your wrist your arm will be pushed down. Kinesiology measures the resistance. How much force has to be used, it is different if you are telling the truth or telling an untruth. As an example, if the day is Wednesday and you say it's Saturday, your arm will collapse easily. If you then say, it's Wednesday you will be able to apply more resistance. It can be done in many ways, including holding objects or even books to determine their level of truth.

In his book *Power vs Force, The Hidden Determinants of Human Behaviour*, Dr David R. Hawkins, M. D., Phd, provides his findings from kinesiology tests on many thousands of people from all walks of life and differing cultures.

From this research, Hawkins has built the 'Map of Consciousness'. The YouTube video link below is Hawkins describing each level.

<u>David Hawkins explains the Scale of Consciousness</u>

I use the 'Log' scale as a reference to our vibrational level. The more internally congruent the higher up the vibrational ladder we go.

Sadly according to Hawkins 85 per cent of the population are below 200. Only 15 per cent of the population are above 200.

Also according to Hawkins a thought that emanates from a consciousness level of 100, living in fear, can be measured with a power between $10^{-800 \text{ million}}$ to $10^{-700 \text{ million}}$ microwatts. It is between 700 and 800 million zero's after the decimal point.

On the other hand a loving thought at the consciousness level of 500 will measure approximately $10^{-35 \text{million}}$ microwatts. This in comparison is only 35 million zero's behind the decimal point. So although again it is infinitesimally small, it is considerably larger than a negative thought. So much larger in fact that a loving thought is so much stronger it will counter 750,000 individuals having a fearful thought.

I will come back to this in Part 3, suffice it to say for now, positive thinking is important to lift yourself up the vibrational ladder, forgiveness at 350 is a very powerful indeed.

Map of Consciousness©

God View	Life View	Level	Log	Emotion	Process
Self	Is	Enlightenment	1000 -700	Ineffable	Pure Consciousness
All-being	Perfect	Peace	600	Bliss	Illumination
One	Complete	Joy	540	Serenity	Transfiguration
Loving	Benign	**Love**	500	Reverence	Revelation
Wise	Meaningful	Reason	400	Understand'g	Abstraction
Merciful	Harmonious	Acceptance	350	**Forgiveness**	Transcendence
Inspiring	Hopeful	Willingness	310	Optimism	Intention
Enabling	Satisfactory	Neutrality	250	Trust	Release
Permitting	Feasible	Courage	200	Affirmation	Empowerment
Level of Truth ↑					
Level of Falsehood ↓					
Indifferent	Demanding	Pride	175	Scorn	Inflation
Vengeful	Antagonistic	Anger	150	Hate	Aggression
Denying	Disappointing	Desire	125	Craving	Enslavement
Punitive	Frightening	Fear	100	Anxiety	Withdrawal
Disdainful	Tragic	Grief	75	Regret	Despondency
Condem'g	Hopeless	Apathy	50	Despair	Abdication
Vindictive	Evil	Guilt	30	Blame	Destruction
Despising	Miserable	Shame	20	Humiliation	Elimination

6 Nirvana

After my initial meeting with Russell and the wonderful people at the Buddhist Society I attended twice a week for 12 years. Russell who at 93 is amazingly nimble was not educated, however he is a man of great intelligence and deeply profound wisdom.

Russell taught me to meditate, the art of mindfulness and to ponder. I began to recognise very subtle differing sensations and feelings created by consciousness. We discussed differing dimensions of reality. The topics were endless and fascinating.

Buddhism is not a religion, not a belief system like Christianity or Islam, it doesn't counter or compete with religion. Many who attended the Buddhist Society also attended churches, mosques and synagogues.

The origins of Buddhism date back to 400 BC. The basic concept is to experience consciousness, to understand the thinking and unconscious mind. Learning comes through personal experience derived from meditation.

Russell advised me not to study Buddhism, nor to read about it. He said, "Words cannot describe true meaning, they are only an interpretation. The only way to know is to experience. Whatever you are doing is providing the experience, so just do what you do."

The point being that our language is a lamentably blunt instrument when it comes to trying to describe an experience like being one with the universe. Language is constructed around our five senses, once we move outside that realm, we are literally lost for words.

This may seem ironic considering I'm expressing myself in this written form and why I've favoured the videos on YouTube. How could I express what Sir Ken Robinson does? His energy comes through beyond the words; it's how he says them, the vibration.

This is also very true about a wonderfully courageous Harvard Neuro-anatomist, Dr Jill Bolte Taylor. Another YouTube TED Video.

<u>Stroke of insight - Jill Bolte Taylor</u> (18 minutes)

Taylor had a massive stroke in the left hemisphere of her brain. It should have and nearly did kill her. It took her eight years to fully recover and tell her story. Taylor explains her experience from the initial identification, as a brain scientist, that she was having a stroke, through the loss of brain functions to an out of the body experience and back.

Her book, *A Stroke of Insight* provides a lot more information than the video of the terrible experience she went through.

Taylor's story is different to that of people who have had NDEs as she explains her journey from a scientist's perspective. What I find particularly interesting is her recognition of the energy and not the physical form of people, she saw Doctors and nurses as energy beings.

Without having to experience what Taylor had to endure, I have been to the same place as her so every time I watch her video, and I've watched it many times as it's the subject of a talk I give, it always brings tears to my eyes. Connecting to the emotion of someone's feeling is a real connection. Too often we focus on the words, we must look deeper into the feeling to understand the true meaning.

The reason I connect so strongly with Taylor is that in February 2007 I experienced a state of sheer bliss like the one she describes. It was off-the-scale scale bliss that I describe as Nirvana and it came at an odd moment; I was not in a meditative, calm or relaxed state, at all.

Paris

Zulf and Mike, two friends and business colleagues and I were in the Tokiama Restaurant in Paris. The restaurant was reasonably busy, it was a Saturday night and we finally sat down at a round table around 10pm, Zulf to my right, Mike to my left.

I was agitated. It had taken us more than two hours to find the Tokiama and I was hungry. I was irritated by the delay in getting to the restaurant, by the fact we hadn't eaten since noon and because Zulf and Mike had been arguing over something I considered trivial. So I was far from calm, far from a meditative state.

As we sat down I ask Zulf to "read my mind". We'd previously attended an NLP course together and practiced mind reading, at which we'd been pretty successful. My intention was for Zulf to understand I was less than happy, in fact very unhappy.

At the very moment I asked the question, my mind said silently to me, "what am I?" It was a question I'd often pondered but a thought so Zulf could not possibly have heard it. His response to my verbal question was spontaneous and he just looked at me and said, "You are light."

Zulf later told me the words just came out of his mouth, he didn't know where they came from. However at that moment my world changed. In Taylor's terms, I stepped into the right hemisphere of my brain and left the left behind. What happened next was very unusual for me and for those that witnessed it.

I felt shivers through my body and it just kept happening, a continuous pleasurable warm tingling sensation, like electricity running through me. It was very pleasant, as if I was buzzing, down my back, through my arms, in my hands, my legs, my feet, everywhere. I began to gently shake as my internal energy rose, I felt wonderful, truly wonderful.

I felt I could achieve anything, I was 'in the zone', on fire. I felt a moment of real power as my internal energy continued to rise. Then I slumped back in my chair, dropped my chopsticks, closed my eyes to enter a different dimension, one of sheer bliss. "What joy, what joy," I said.

I was aware of my body but somehow became detached from it, I lost my sense of self, all those previous feelings running through my body had gone. I felt sheer bliss, an overdose of joy. Mike said later that I'd left. He said my body was there but it was a shell. "You weren't in it Dave," he said.

I had no appreciation of time it didn't exist. There was no now and then, it was timelessness, joy a truly blissful state. It's like loving every soul in the universe and having it reflected back tenfold, it's infinite love, pure bliss.

Mike said it lasted around 20 minutes but to me it was an instant and eternity combined. Again words cannot explain timelessness or how I felt, which was blissful, utterly boundless joy.

Mike and Zulf were speaking to me and holding my hands, saying, "Dave, come back" but although I heard the words they didn't register, they were not for me. I was somewhere else and there was more than a reticence to acknowledge anything because nothing was all there is; a nothingness that is everything. Yes it does sound contradictory but that is what it was.

At one point, I opened my eyes but sight was too limiting. What I saw was not real it was an illusion. Sight presented objects that have boundaries – but there are no boundaries, so I closed my eyes again and went straight back to my new reality. It meant so much more, had more meaning, without any meaning at all, yet it was still more real, it had quality, real quality, refinement, comfort, joy, bliss, utter bliss. This was an experience that cannot be described, however when I hear others attempt to describe their experiences of Nirvana I recognise the state and their difficulty in finding the words.

Eventually, I opened my eyes again and this time I found sight and objects, funny. I knew the things I could see did not exist, so again I closed them and went straight back into this new reality. Then I felt something wanted me to return to the physical world but I had no intention of so doing. Why leave a place of pure bliss?

Zulf wanted me to return so he slapped my face several times but it had no effect, I hardly felt anything more of a wipe than a strike. He said he didn't feel he could hit me harder in the middle of a restaurant.

I didn't want to open my eyes so I slapped my own face and felt nothing. If only there had been cameras! Mike didn't believe anyone could hit themselves as hard I did, I remember it well, I didn't feel anything, no pain, just a slight sensation hence I could hit myself very hard, it didn't seem like me hitting me. Interestingly there was never a mark left.

Finally I opened my eyes and had to concentrate hard to keep them open. The scene in front of me was so unreal; it was false. As I looked around, the bliss disappeared and although I was far from back in the physical world, I had returned sufficiently to stand up as we had to leave the restaurant, people around were uncomfortable about what they'd seen. Well I can appreciate that!

"This is a true and accurate description of what I witnessed in Paris."

Zulf Ali, Rochdale, Manchester.

Outside, the walls of buildings didn't appear real and touching things felt odd. Why was I feeling a barrier when I 'knew' there wasn't one? I was lifting one foot up and moving it forward to propel myself in nothing, how utterly futile it felt and yet so funny, it was hilarious. Movement had 'here and there,' it created time and distance, I sat on the pavement. There was no point to it I couldn't associate with the physical 3D world, at all.

Sight, sound, smell, taste and touch all have boundaries, they have 'before' and 'after', 'up' and 'down'. They all have limits and opposites like black and white, soft and hard, hot and cold. Our senses show us distance and measure time, this creates the perception of separation.

This other place is everything other than what we can see, feel, taste, smell or hear, and that is infinitely more. It is a place of pure quality, everything is harmonious, perfection, infinite love.

So what happened?

As I began this amazing experience I went through a few stages. First I had the shivering, then a buzzing and being 'in the zone'. This was followed by a feeling that I could achieve anything before, wham, my vibration went to at least the relative number of 600 on David Hawkins 'Map of Consciousness'.

I've had the 'knowing I can achieve anything', experience before. When it comes there is no desire to do anything, as everything that is, I already felt I had.

As I went up the vibrational ladder, I left the 3D, with all its attributes, behind. This started with the feeling of excitement, being in the zone, but what happened next I believe was a dimensional shift, my vibration went through the roof.

The feeling that I could achieve anything, or more precisely, instinctively a knowing I could, with no desire to do anything at all, is above my interpretation of the 6D as being one with the universe. This was a non-physical experience, so for now I'll call it the seventh dimension.

There was no 3D or 5D material world in which to impose my will and I had no desire to impose my will, I'd left that behind. I knew I had everything there was to have, so there was no need for, or to do, anything. However this state didn't include bliss or love, I believe that comes with the next dimensional shift, that I'll call the eighth but that's my interpretation, I really have no idea, again no passport control.

When we start to consider, as mathematicians and quantum physicists do, that there are more than three dimensions, is it so difficult to accept that some people can experience other dimensions through altered states of consciousness? Indeed, like myself, some people already have done it but they may not appreciate what it is that happened to them.

> It was not possible to form the laws of Quantum Mechanics in a fully consistent way without reference to the consciousness of the observer.
>
> The very study of the external world led to the conclusion that the content of consciousness was the ultimate reality.
>
> Eugene Paul Wigner
> Winner of Nobel Prize for Physics 1963
> Ex-President of the American Physics Society

In the DVD *What the 'Bleep' do we know?* Dr Andrew Newberg describes altered state of consciousness and he explains that many people have had similar experiences to mine. Newberg describes how we perceive these states to be more real than the physical world. Unlike a dream, which seems real during the dream but we know it to be a dream when we wake. These altered states of consciousness still feel more real than the physical when we return. Something I can vouch for and it's reassuring to know I'm not alone.

My Nirvana experience was not visual because the visual world was unreal. The 'in the body' experience is a lower vibration, whereas the, 'out of body', experience is a significantly higher one. Mike said I'd left my body but I was in it, I couldn't have left because there was no 'here and there', nowhere to go. I'd entered a higher vibrational rate that could not be recognised by his.

I have asked Zulf to say to me "you are light" many times but sadly nothing happens. However the experience didn't end when we left the restaurant.

We left Paris on Sunday evening and I was still not quite myself, I felt odd, as if in a half way house between what I was seeing and how I felt. I was however able to function normally and on the outside all probably looked fine.

Episode with a treadmill

The following day I went to Cardiac Rehabilitation in Wilmslow, a town in Cheshire. I'd been going since my return from Spain and I was nearing the end of the six-month programme. Although I didn't know it then I now feel I'd already fixed my heart as I found the programme easy. I could easily run on a treadmill for a prolonged period. This particular Monday I was jogging away happily when a nurse came over and asked how I was, "fine" I said. She followed up with another question, "did you do anything this weekend?"

My mind went straight back to the experience in Paris and again time just stopped, I stopped, the treadmill didn't, I shot backwards. The next thing I recall is being on the floor a crumpled mess with nurses around me taking my pulse, my blood pressure and listening to my heart. I couldn't focus, nothing seemed real, I was confused, what just happened? Words were being spoken but I didn't seem to appreciate them and couldn't respond, I felt very disorientated; everything just seemed so odd, so different.

Eventually I was allowed to stand up, I've no idea how long this took but all the measurements taken seemed to provide the nurses with the confidence that this was nothing to do with my heart, so I went to the changing rooms. I sat down still confused and asked myself, 'what on earth is going on?" I just sat and tried to focus, the more I tried and failed the more distressed I became, as I couldn't. Nothing was real, was I real? It was a nightmare. After a while a thought came to mind, "ring Melody", having no other options I did.

I'd met Melody on my initial NLP training course, our introduction could be considered just a little odd.

It was the second day of a seven-day residential course; there were 18 of us in six groups of three in a large rectangular room. I was in one corner with two others, I had my back to the room. Suddenly a huge negative emotion flooded through me and I immediately broke down in tears, floods of tears and I had absolutely no idea why. Needless to say it brought the procedure to an abrupt stop as my two colleagues looked at me totally dumbfounded.

Michelle came over, took one look at me and said, "turn around", which I did to see Melody diagonally opposite in the corner facing out into the room. She was in floods of tears, two other delegates kneeling in front of her holding her hands. I looked at her and recognised I was experiencing her emotional state.

Eventually Melody settled down and so did I and we continued with the course. When the mid morning coffee break arrived I sought out Melody, an odd introduction, "we seem to have something in common", I said. We chatted and became good friends and still are to this day.

Melody has psychic abilities and see's things and has other insights that I've found very helpful, she was an obvious choice when seeking the help I needed.

So I'm sat in the changing rooms and the thought of speaking to Melody came to mind and I rang her. Fortunately she answered almost immediately and I told her about the previous three days and my episode with the treadmill. Her response was not expected.

Melody started shouting at me, calling me an idiot and other even more derogatory terms flowed from her. I felt my energy collapse, totally. I felt myself shrink, as if I was a balloon deflating and with that deflation I re-associated within my body, I was back in the physical reality of the 3D.

Eventually Melody stopped and enquired "Dave?" Her tone changed as she continued, "are you still there?" I said "yes" and she told me I must ground myself more, something I was still to learn. That verbal dressing down had brought me back to earth, never has a telling off been so helpful.

Our childhood 'dressing downs' may be supressed and believed forgotten, but they are held in our unconscious, they are part of our baggage, they hold us down from the higher vibrational rates I've experienced. As Bolte Taylor says somewhat jovially, that the stroke caused her to lose the "37 years of emotional baggage" that was held in the part of her brain affected by the stroke.

We all have baggage, stacks of it. Don't think that, just because we're older now, we've dealt with it. Not unless you actually have taken the time and effort needed to deal with it through a method such as therapy. Yes a therapist would say that I know but it's true. In 2007, I was carrying a lot more baggage than I realised so why did the Nirvana experience happen to me?

I believe it was planned and that I didn't have any choice. We believe in free will but perhaps some are not as free to choose our path as we may think. I certainly feel I'm not as free as I'd thought and Zak has confirmed that. He has explained to me that when we chose a spiritual path then we agree to a reduction in our free will.

When we have dispensed with all our baggage we can then transcend this 3D illusion, just as Taylor did when she stepped from the left to the right hemisphere of her brain. There are however other constraints and these can come from our soul purpose. We have other things to consider.

As I said in the introduction, we are multi-dimensional beings. This has been said many times but I interpret what happened to Taylor and I as entering another dimension of reality.

For Taylor and myself this experience was spontaneous but it is also possible to attain an altered state of consciousness through intention, solitude and meditation.

Bubbles

Paul was one of the people at the Buddhist Society who listened to my 'one with the universe' story. He understood what I was talking about through study but hadn't experienced anything like it himself.

Paul decided to take a year out and go to a Buddhist Temple to discover more about the tradition. It wasn't until several years later, well after his return, that we had an opportunity to chat. I asked him what his journey was like as I was considering doing something similar myself.

Paul said that after a day or two of settling in and getting up at 4am for meditation, followed by a simple breakfast (he thought he may starve) and chores, he was sent to sit in the mouth of a cave overlooking a forest. Just sit until sunset, he was told. On his return he was asked what he saw.

He'd been looking at the same scene for hours and hours so he described as best he could the wonderful trees, shrubs, colours, noises, etc. "Very good," he was told.

The following morning was the same. Off he went back to the cave. "I must have missed something," he thought to himself and this time studied the forest more carefully. On his return he was more careful about the detail and again he was told, "Very good."

The third day was the same again. Day followed day, week followed week and month followed month. The same routine for nearly three months. Paul told me he was getting heartily sick of the forest; he wondered what on earth he was doing there and why he had been so stupid to come in the first place. You can imagine, well I can, it'd drive me crazy.

Then one day, he was so utterly bored that he just settled and he started seeing bubbles coming out of the ground. They got bigger as they rose up and then just disappeared as if pricked with a pin, like bubbles in a soda. Then there were more and more until the whole forest was full of bubbles. He sat mesmerised.

On his return he was greeted with the same question, "What did you see?" This time a silence before the simple word; "bubbles".

Paul never went back to the cave, although he visited the forest often. After this his days were filled with discussion of the experience of consciousness.

I was fascinated and now even keener to go myself but Paul said, "Dave you don't need to go, you've been there." 'I haven't seen bubbles,' I thought but that wasn't the point.

No two people have the same experience of three-dimensional reality, so why would an experience of expanded awareness or altered state of consciousness be the same for any two people? Does it need to be? Does it have to be different? It may be the same, but equally it may be different.

Paul said to me very kindly, "the only reason I went was because of you. When I listened to your story I just knew I had to make the trip I'd been considering for years." I felt quite emotional about that short statement and humbled to have played a role in instigating such a transformational event in someone's life.

This gave even greater clarity to Russell's advice about not studying Buddhism. It'd be others' experiences I'd want to duplicate and if I couldn't then I'd feel I was missing something or failed in some way.

Paul's story though has a lesson for us all in letting go of our perceptions, our conditioning, our thoughts and beliefs. As Taylor describes, these are our left brain, thinking attributes.

If I was going to rebrand Buddhism, give it a facelift and bring it into the 21st Century marketing world (forgetting for a moment that marketing is a big part of our problem), I'd call it:

'Training in Inter-Dimensional Travel'

You don't have to be a saint or become a hermit on a hillside who does nothing but meditate for days to recognise what life really is. You just have to recognise what you really are, which is consciousness living a 3D experience for a reason. Once that small seed begins it's growth then your journey has begun.

It's our programming, our conditioning, our baggage we need to address and that's an individual assignment. There are many who can help but first you must decide you want to make the journey.

The things I've experienced and I'm writing about have been spoken of for centuries. Some quantum physicists are now corroborating this, as are some neuroscientists and microbiologists, all I'm doing is tying things up as I've had the experiences to prove them right.

However we still come up against people who are unwilling to accept experiences such as mine. Nor will they accept that ancient cultures knew more about reality than Western science. Acceptance of this challenges materialism at its very core and the whole structure of Western society.

I spent years with the experience of 'one with the universe', before I had it explained to me by Russell. Where does one go to discuss such an experience, a church, a doctor or psychologist? I tried all of these but was more likely to be handed pills, told it was stress or a trick of the mind. No matter what I say, many people will maintain the view that what I experienced was just a trick of the mind and I cannot prove otherwise, however there are many others who have the same or similar experience so it's evidential.

Medicate or understand

I wonder how many people are being medicated because they have had experiences that traditional medical science cannot understand? Experiences that could be explained with the understanding that we are multi-dimensional beings, not just biological machines that happen to be born then die, end of story. Actually death is the beginning of the story but we are delving into the, which came first, the 'chicken or egg' scenario.

The link between education, psychology and pharmaceutical companies is not a healthy one. Pharmaceutical companies are measured on the stock market, they have shareholders and their business is making money by selling drugs. Their business is not curing people it's maintaining them. They have massive financial clout and use it.

How many children are medicated when in reality they should be understood? As a five year old, I'd probably be called delusional. It's more than possible that these children are not ill, it's our society that is ill. We lack understanding due to our Level 1 thinking. This keeps medical science in a box and prevents the acceptance of anything outside society's accepted norms. Lock together education, pharmaceuticals, doctors and the stock market, that is one 'hell' of a lobby group against what I am saying.

We need to stop thinking of ourselves as biological machines that just happen to have minds and recognise we are consciousness with capabilities well beyond the range of our imaginations. Consciousness that is presently experiencing being physical for the purpose of learning.

The accumulation of wealth and assets is not intelligent. It's 3D materialism that has got us in this environmental, social and political mess. We need to become more intelligent and a lot wiser.

7 Separation

I'd known my now ex-wife Steph since she was 14, then she was my best mate's neighbour's girlfriend. She is eight years younger than me and when I was in my early twenties that's quite a big gap so I'd never considered her as a potential girlfriend.

It was 1978 and I'd left England to work in Abu Dhabi. After a year I was home on leave, things had changed, Steph was now 18.

I'd only been back a few days and was at a bar with friends. Steph was also there and she came over to chat. A couple of days later, she rang me and we arranged to go out the following Saturday night. On our first date, we were driving into Manchester on the A34 and stopped at Parrs Wood traffic lights. As I sat waiting for the lights to change I put my hand out to hold hers. In that instant it just came to me that I would marry her. I was somewhat surprised that such a thought would come when I really hardly knew her. However the next thing my mind said to me was, "behave yourself, don't mess this up". From that moment I was on my very best behaviour.

Just short of two years later, on the 1st of November 1980, we were married.

On our wedding day, just as the reception was about to start, Steph's chief bridesmaid Sandra reminded us of a boy racer incident six years earlier that I'd prefer was totally forgotten. Slightly embarrassed I admitted remembering it and then Sandra said, "It was then that Steph told me she would marry you." Sandra said at that time she found it funny as I was usually seen with trophy-type girls and she thought Steph was far too young for me.

We separated 32 years later in January 2012 and divorced in November 2014.

We have three wonderful children and remain friends. We now just accept we've become different people. I was no longer the man my wife married. Being friends probably kept us together too long, to cause a split needed something to happen and I did that.

Things came to a head one evening in November 2011 when we went out to dinner with our friends Charlie and Jan. Steph had suggested an Indian restaurant in one of the more expensive areas of Cheshire. We've known Charlie and Jan for over 30 years. We were with them in Spain when I had my heart attack and we went out with them regularly. The atmosphere was light-hearted and jovial, I felt fine as Steph and I walked hand in hand the few hundred metres from the rail station to the restaurant. We sat down and ordered our meals; I ordered a kebab as a starter.

Now I must point out here that I am considered a pretty good barbeque cook. I'd spend many hours preparing and marinating food for barbeques. I often bought meat and spices from Rusholme, a predominately Asian area south of Manchester. On one visit there I had to wait as the lamb chops were being cut so I wandered around the shop, I saw some frozen kebabs, a dozen for only £3 seemed like good value so I bought them. These kebabs were all uniform size about 20cm long and 3cm wide, with an oval hole through the middle, where a skewer had been, they had the obligatory identical diagonal burn marks so they looked like they'd come from a BBQ. They were over priced, as they were more like rubber than meat and were difficult to cut, never mind chew. They were all thrown away.

What was put in front of me at this expensive restaurant was one of these same kebabs. It was like trying to cut through a tyre inner tube and it tasted terrible. I couldn't believe it. Everyone else's starter was fine though, so I excused myself and went to the bathroom.

On the way, I stopped a waiter with the intent of asking him to take the meal away but I hadn't planned to say the words that came out of my mouth, which were, " Take that that fucking awful shit away." I assure you that I don't usually behave like that but I was pretty annoyed. I don't recall the price of the kebab now but I do remember thinking it was expensive for a starter even in an expensive restaurant.

When I returned to the table, I found the offending kebab was still there. Steph said she had told them to leave it. I still have no idea why although I probably should as this set up a chain of events that resulted in our divorce.

At this point I seemed to lose it completely. My peripheral vision turned red. I've heard people say they "saw red', well I actually did. I became tunnel visioned with red mist filling all the surrounding area. Coupled with that I felt claustrophobic and three waiters were now invading my space. I cannot recall what happened but there was a scene and I left the restaurant needing both space and air.

I walked for a mile or so trying to calm myself. I couldn't understand why I had behaved like I had; it was so out of character. After a while, I turned back and found Charlie outside the restaurant looking for me, I'd been gone for well over half an hour. Charlie was quite frank, "Dave you're acting like a prat," he said, "Charlie, that's not helping," I replied. He went back inside and I followed him a few minutes later. Steph was upset and told me to leave so I got a taxi home.

This was the catalyst that caused the separation. At that time the whole thing confused me but now it doesn't. Steph needed something to push her over the edge and I obliged. Buying the frozen kebabs, something I'd never done before, as I make my own, was required to set the scene for the drama that unfolded a few weeks later.

It was the following morning that Steph said she wanted a separation.

We put on an act over Christmas, I was still hoping for reconciliation. However in the first week of January, we went to see our friends and told them together that we were spitting up. We both explained we wanted it to be amicable.

Before we separated I went away for week. Being together was becoming increasingly more stressful. On my return I bought a rather large bouquet of flowers. Steph was out and I left them in the kitchen and went to my home office.

A while later Steph came home and came into my office. As she did I felt a massive shift in my emotional state. I suddenly became very calm and very still, as if all the emotional baggage I was carrying just evaporated. I also felt there was no need for words indeed I didn't have any. Steph then said, "Dave what have you bought the flowers for, it's over."

Then as I looked at her she turned golden yellow. A massive aura about half a metre around her body, it was neon bright it was her emotional field. She then said to me, very calmly and in a very caring and loving manner, "I'm letting you go, I'm setting you free, you are better off without me."

Then a beautiful voice said very softly in my right ear, "Let her go."

I was awestruck, Steph left the room and I remained in that emotionless state for a while longer. I had never seen an aura before and when I did it was so bright. I've never seen it as bright since. As for the voice in my ear, I didn't want to acknowledge that.

I explained what happened to Russell at the Buddhist Society and he said, "You saw her in her angelic state, where she can speak only pure truth." At the time I didn't want to hear this as I was still hoping for reconciliation but never have any words been more truthful.

Despair to Joy in 20 minutes

A few weeks later, I was walking around Poynton Pool and my mood was getting worse and worse. I'd plummeted down the octaves and was at the bottom of the lowest. I became so desperately depressed and so very quickly. I became so low I wasn't previously aware that such a low state of feeling existed. In that state I can understand why people may wish to end their own lives. I felt totally helpless and pleaded with my guides for the help I so desperately needed.

Poynton Pool was frozen over with about 10cm of ice. I considered walking into the middle and jumping up and down until I fell through. Then an acquaintance walked up and engaged me in conversation. On reflection, I wonder if that 'chance' meeting saved my life.

After we finished speaking, I carried on walking home. It was about 20 minutes later when, just as if I was hit by a bolt of lightening I suddenly felt total love for 'All That Is'. This incredible feeling of pure love for everything flowed through me and I felt totally joyous. I was stood outside Poynton Chip Shop, in full view of the people queuing for their lunch, with my arms reaching up to the heavens saying 'thank you'. Moments later I was thinking once again, 'what on earth is going on?'

It took me more than two years to figure it out. A lot is going on and I'm just following the script. Zak's introduction to my guides' communication brought with it the recognition of what happened outside the chip shop.

When I was walking around Poynton Pool, my mind was rehearsing all the negative aspects of my then situation. I was out of work, my marriage had collapsed and I was approaching the dreaded age of 60. I could see no future. My mind was full of negative self-talk. Walking back to the house my mind cleared, I gave it the space to let the guides get through to deliver what I'd asked for over 20 minutes earlier.

A couple of months later I went to Dubai. It was Steph's suggestion and as I had nothing holding me in England, I went. I now realise I was running away but in a direction I had to go.

Queens Golden Jubilee

In June I returned to the UK to the to see the family, it was the week prior to the Queen's Golden Jubilee celebrations. I was in Poynton and I'd invited Steph for lunch. Over conversation she mentioned going to London to see our two sons James and Ben that coming weekend. Coincidently, I had the same plan as my flight back to Dubai was from London on the Sunday night. Steph immediately said, "You go, I can go anytime." I asked why we couldn't go together and she said "no reason", so we did and Sophie and Jamie came from Birmingham. Jamie has now given up cage fighting as Sophie didn't like seeing people hit him.

It was an unusual train journey. We hadn't spent so much time in normal conversation since the previous November before the unfortunate kebab incident. However we do get on well together so we were both able to find it all quite amusing, the conversation was easy and relaxed. It brought a lot back.

It was the wrong time to be travelling in London though. The Queen was taking a boat ride down the River Thames and security was extreme. We couldn't get south of the river and ended up in a bar waiting for Her Majesty to get out of the way. I felt the energy between us had settled a lot, we were light-hearted.

The family were together for a weekend and that was very nice indeed. Steph and I shared a room in James's apartment Steph on the sofa and me on the floor and spoke about the separation.

We discussed how we were both dealing with the circumstances we found ourselves in. Steph said she didn't know why she was doing it; she just felt she had to. She didn't like splitting the family or the impact it was having on the children, or for that matter on her. She told me she was suffering but deep inside, in her heart, she knew she was doing the right thing.

The following morning things were more difficult, Steph was emotional and found it difficult to leave for Euston Station to get the train home. The family time together had brought back too much.

I absolutely hate seeing Steph distressed but there was little I could do. She left for Euston early afternoon. That night I was due to fly back to Dubai.

When I got to Heathrow Airport, I rang her. She was still confused and still just a little upset. We talked for over an hour and I nearly missed my flight. I do not know if Steph ever considered asking me to return but if she had I feel I would not now be living in Peru.

Although Steph had rejected my spiritual path, she is following her own. She is listening to herself at a deep, fundamental, intuitive Level 5. As she had been when, nearly 40 years earlier she told Sandra she would marry me.

Divorced

In early 2014, I was again back to the UK and this time I took the signed divorce papers to her. How things can change because now we were planning to go out for dinner to celebrate. Ki had been right, I was completely at ease with the divorce.

We didn't go out in the end, staying in to celebrate with two bottles of wine and a take-away.

Steph's laptop was quite old, slow and regularly freezing so I bought her a divorce present, an Apple MacBook Air. The Apple salesman at The Trafford Centre, a mall near Manchester, did not believe I was buying a MacBook Air as a divorce present. I tried to convince him but he wouldn't believe me.

Spiritual Development

In her book *Transformed by the Light*, Australian researcher Cherie Sutherland has identified the impact that near death experiences (NDEs) have on people. I haven't gone through an NDE, although being 'one with the universe' felt as if I had.

Cherie's work has been substantiated by other studies, Ring (1980 and 1984) and Atwater (1988). According to these studies, the changes reported by people who've experienced NDE's include:

1   A universal belief in life after death,
2   80 per cent now believed in re-incarnation,
3   A total absence of fear of death,
4   A shift from organised religion to personal spiritual practice,
5   A statistically significant increase in psychic sensitivity,
6   A more positive view of self and others,
7   An increased desire for solitude,
8   An increased sense of purpose,
9   A lack of interest in material success,
10   50 per cent experience a major difficulty in a previously close relationship,
11   An increase in health consciousness,
12   Most drank less alcohol,
13   Almost all gave up smoking,
14   Most gave up prescription drugs,
15   Most watched less TV and read fewer newspapers,
16   An increased interest in alternative healing,
17   50 per cent go through a major change in career in which they moved towards helping others.

Since my boulder's last appearance I changed in the same way. Almost all of these categories apply to me. The exception is my interest in current affairs; I continue to read newspapers.

Obviously a divorce fits within the description for number 10, a 'major difficulty in a previously close relationship'. Also, I think that seeing Steph's angelic aura, fits within number five, an increase in psychic sensitivity, which is something that continues to develop.

Wendy

During the difficult early days of the separation, I was counselling Wendy who had terminal cancer. I really enjoyed our Friday afternoons, we had a lot of fun and laughter. One afternoon though I was feeling quite distressed and I didn't want Wendy to pick up on my state.

As I parked my car, I asked my guides for help over the next three hours and as I walked up the drive I again felt a shift in my emotional state, just like I had when I'd seen Steph's aura.

Wendy took one look at me and said, "Dave, what's wrong? It's not you, who are you?" A question I didn't know how to answer. "You're frightening me," she said. So I sat some distance away. I had no words and felt emotionless, no desire to speak. Then I said, "It is me Wendy but I do feel different, I have no words." We sat and looked at each other for around five minutes before Wendy said, "There are no words are there, it's beautiful."

Wendy didn't recognise me because my emotional and my mental field was different to what she was accustomed to.

However, Wendy then shifted her state and joined mine. As I now write about this, I realise that Wendy's experience of an altered state of consciousness that day was a marvellous thing for someone who was facing death.
Wendy's Return

Wendy came back to see me about six months after she died. I was on my past life regression course and I woke early. I suddenly saw a cup of coffee in front of me. It was real enough but not a physical cup of coffee. The image grew bigger and the coffee was sat on a coffee table. Then it grew even bigger and there was a sofa behind the coffee table. At this point I recognised the scene, it was Wendy's lounge. Every time I went to see Wendy she made me a cup of coffee.

Then the scene expanded again and stood at the doorway was a beautiful goddess of a woman. She was tall and slender with long golden hair held high with a headband with a large green emerald and flowing down her shoulders in ringlets. She was wearing a silver grey dress split at the hip and held with a golden broach. She had a perfect figure and was showing me her left leg. She was absolutely gorgeous.

Then she morphed onto the sofa and changed into Wendy sitting as she did on my left. She looked at me and said, "Tell Mark I'm okay, tell him I'm fine." The next moment, the scene vanished.

Mark is Wendy's husband and a scientist who openly admits he is not in the slightest spiritual. However when I told him the story he couldn't help his eyes welling up as he said to me, "That means so much. Wendy had such a fear of dying and what she would find on the other side."

There is nothing to be fearful of on the other side there is no divine retribution, it's a place of peace, harmony and love just love, that is all we'll find there.

Leonora

I'd arranged to have a coffee with my friend Leonora at JamaicaBlue cafe, in Ibn Battuta Mall, Dubai. As she sat down, I had another altered state that I will call a 'shutdown' and just looked at Leonora and said, "I have no words."

Leonora immediately retorted, "I wish you'd told me earlier I'd have brought a friend," which I still find amusing.

I just sat in a completely still and emotionless state; Leonora just looked at me and there was no conversation. After a few minutes, Leonora said, "There are no words are there, it's beautiful." Later she explained how calm she became, a whole new level of calm that she'd never previously experienced.

We recognise people's energy fields and notice when someone has that black cloud but we also know when someone lifts our spirits. Our vibrational level impacts others. I've no idea why this happened with Leonora other than she is on a wonderful journey of her own and this was just a little demonstration of what was to come.

We've all been there.

I believe we have all experienced something similar although maybe we don't recognise it. The experience may not necessarily be the same degree or depth as the way I describe a shutdown.

Have you ever been with someone, a partner, lying together still and calm, doing nothing, no TV, no music, nothing. Not thinking and not wanting to speak or move? Feeling that speaking would break the magic. Feeling that you are so 'together'.

Can you recall a moment, with a new lover maybe, when you went into that zone?

I can remember and I know how beautiful it is. It's an altered state to the state of which we are far too accustomed. It is when we are truly living in the moment. Becoming pure observers and recognising we are one. This is a state of 'being' and not 'doing'. It's a real shift in our vibration.

Our education system and culture respect and emphasise the importance of 'doing' while not recognising 'being'. Being is where our happiness lies and it's en route to higher vibration, 'being' enables us to recognise our intuition, our path and our destiny.

If Steph hadn't listened to her inner self; her intuition and had persevered with our marriage, I'd be stuck in a hole so deep I don't even want to consider it. In fact, what I later discovered in a conversation with Zak, it would have literally killed me.

Part 2

Dubai

Not what I expected

8 A new chapter

Nothing was happening for me in England. My marriage had dissolved, I was out of work and I felt no one really understood me - not that I could blame anyone for that as I didn't understand myself.

My support group was close to zero because the few friends I had were a distance away. Fortunately money wasn't a problem as Steph and I had split the proceeds from our house sale.

This was a low point in my life and the experience around Poynton Pool had really made me aware of how low I was. The moments of utter joy 20 minutes later had left me totally confused and I felt that experience was now long gone.

At the time I was taking an NLP Master Practitioner course and that did help. I had some brilliant therapy from Michelle with whom I'd previously done my NLP Practitioner and Hypnotherapy training but even that had little impact. On the outside I may have looked fine, inside I was in utter turmoil.

Steph suggested I went to spend sometime in Dubai with her very close friend Sue but that didn't seem to resonate and I just stagnated. It was about a month later when waiting for Sophie in a car park in Birmingham I suddenly got the urge to go to Dubai. Just sitting and waiting I let go, when I did I gave the space to let the message in.

I immediately rang Sue and within a few days I was in Dubai. 'A new start, fresh beginning,' I thought. The problem I didn't realise I had was that I was still carrying old ideas.

The first few months I was still in 'old Dave' mode. Commercially minded, I was seeking a big job with huge responsibility and an equally huge salary. I had some great interviews and great feedback but nothing actually happened, as I later discovered and what should have been obvious, I was too old. Time passed and after a few months my spirits began to recover, being out of England was good for me but work was still elusive.

I started a few things helping others and wondered every time if this was it but nothing ever got past the initial stages, it became a pattern. Weeks became months and soon it became a year. I really wondered what on earth I would do with the rest of my life.

Sue had introduced me to a number of people in Dubai, one of whom had a dramatic impact.

Carol runs her own NLP training business and travels a lot doing motivational speaking. She was heading off on another trip when at the last minute her house sitter let her down and she needed someone to look after her cats. She asked me if I would spend a week at her villa in Arabian Ranches, one of the more premium areas of Dubai. 'Why not,' I thought.

I went to see Carol to learn my cat-sitting duties and we started talking about books. Carol recommended a few that she had and in that week she was away, I read and read. There was a world out there that I had no awareness of and I learnt so much. Amongst others I read Gregg Braden's *Divine Matrix*, a fascinating book.

A week or so after Carol's return, she rang me and asked if I'd read Michael Newton's book, *'Journey of the Souls'*. I hadn't so during the conversation I searched Amazon and downloaded it onto my iPad. The following day Carol rang me again and asked what I thought of the book. I hadn't even looked at it. She said, "I'm going, I'm going." I had absolutely no idea what she was talking about but thought I'd better read the book quickly, and I did.

This was the beginning of a new chapter, the fresh start. Here the old ideas were not just put to bed, they were buried so deep they would never be unearthed.

The Michael Newton Institute (MNI) in San Francisco has regressed over 12,000 people back to their last incarnation, through the death scene into the spirit realms. Regardless of religion, or being an atheist, the process we all go through according to the MNI research is the same. There may be some cosmetic differences between different people, however the process is fundamentally the same.

I read '*Journey of the Souls*' and Michael Newton's other two books in less than a week. I was enthralled and decided to go with Carol for the soul regression I discovered she was speaking about a week earlier. I wanted to do a soul regression myself to discover what my life purpose was, indeed that I had one.

As it turns out, Carol didn't go and I went to see Christine Pearson in London alone. Christine had trained in regression at MNI and the date was set for 26 February 2013.

Before I went I'd already decided I wanted to become a 'soul regressionalist' and so contacted the MNI. Their next course was in November so I booked on it. Reading the course prerequisites, I needed to have done a past life regression course and I had 10 months to find a course acceptable to them.

I spoke to Christine and she recommended Andy Tomlinson in Dorset, England. As if by sheer good fortune his next course began on the 28 February. I was on it!

Andy runs the 'Past Life Regression Academy' and was also trained by Michael Newton although in many respects Andy has developed things further since Michael retired. MNI confirmed I needed to do only his first four-day module and I'd be accepted on the course.

Everything looked set, I had a new direction, I felt energised in a way I'd not felt for years. I had an internal buzz and sense of inner comfort and wellbeing. But there were still a few experiences to have in Dubai before setting off once again for England.

Nicola Pierson – A Psychic with punch.

Carol had recommended Nicola saying she was exceptional. I was to discover how true that is. I booked a session with her before I left Dubai for London.

Nicola explained it took her around 20 minutes to 'tune in' so we chatted and then she said calmly, "I'm getting it now." Nicola told me about my guides and one in particular who would help me in the future with my healing. She saw my dad in spirit and said he was "chuckling", which he did and she told me a lot more. There was so much detail about the people around me. She told me about my heart attack in 2007, how serious it was and how I'm fully recovered. She said I'd be divorced in the middle of the following year and I'd be happy about it. At that time I was still hoping for reconciliation.

She said I had a bright future with no worries that everything would work out well for me from hereon in. Although the cynic in me says that there had to be a positive following the negative of my divorce.

Towards the end of the session, I explained I was off to London for a soul regression and then to Dorset for a course and that later I was going San Francisco to learn about soul regression.

Nicola said, "Tell me about this first thing, how did you meet?" I began an explanation but Nicola interrupted and said, "That woman will change your life, you will not be the same when you return to Dubai after seeing her, what's next?"

I began to explain about Andy Tomlinson and again Nicola interrupted, "He's part of it, he's part of the change, you will be different when you come back, what's next?"

I then began to explain about my trip to San Francisco and again Nicola interrupted and said, "No, that's not going to happen, you're not going there." 'Little do you know,' I thought. The whole reason for the course with Andy Tomlinson was to enable me to go to MNI.

That very same evening I got an email from the MNI postponing the November course and asking to reschedule in early 2014. I intended to but events overtook me and in the end I didn't follow up.

As it transpires, everything Nicola said has come to fruition, I didn't see her again until August 2014 when I went for another specific reason.

Christine Pearson – the journey begins.

To say my expectations were high would be an understatement and we know it is wrong to have expectations, however I had an excuse - Nicola set them. However my expectations were exceeded. The regression took three hours and it was incredible.

It was easy for Christine to put me into a hypnotic trance, as I've had so much hypnosis and I love it, being in trance is a beautiful experience.

Christine asked my guides to take me to a previous life that would have significance for the present one.

I was shown the scene, inside what seemed to be a shop and soon recognised I was an apothecary and it was in 1456, the year was specific. I was particularly grumpy as I was far too busy mixing medicine with many people demanding more. I felt I was in France. It was all very clear, I was wearing a leather apron and people were banging on the door and at windows looking in.

Being an apothecary was very pertinent indeed although it was two years before I'd find out just how pertinent.

Christine then asked me to go to my previous incarnation to this present one. I immediately jumped to a scene that was known to me. It was WWII, I was an American seaman killed in a blast on a ship, something to do with being hit in my chest, my body died instantly.

The soul left the body and I followed its path into the light without resistance, there was nothing holding me to the physical world and I went into the soul world very quickly.

I felt myself being cleansed. I seemed to have four energies around me and they seemed to be going through a process of stroking me whilst all singing in harmony, not words but rhythmic melodies. They started at my head and worked down and as they did I saw myself change colour. I started as a very light grey and ended up a pale pink, with grey dust on the floor around my feet.

One of the energies gathered the dust and it formed a large ball about 60 centimetres in diameter and they took it away. Christine told me to follow it and it seemed to be put into a massive cabinet. I can only describe it as being something with many small doors, like a bank of school lockers.

My grey dust was put in the bottom left locker and then seemingly taken out of the top right one, but as it was I noticed it was now pure white. This pure white energy was given back to me and as it was I felt uplifted, as if the voltage had been turned up on a filament light bulb, just that little bit brighter.

I didn't meet anyone I knew, as all showed themselves in energy not human form.

Christine asked about my present incarnation, when did I enter the body? I explained that as a spirit I came into the human body at five months gestation for an introduction I don't know how long I stayed. I returned to fully integrate at seven months. I came with 35 per cent of my soul energy and Christine asked if this was my idea or by agreement, I wanted to bring more but by agreement it was left at 35 per cent.

The scene was beautiful, everyone was happily light hearted and always laughing and singing. It's all fun and laughter up there, a lovely place to be.

Christine asked for me to be taken to the Elders, as this was the objective to discover my soul purpose, but nothing happened. I asked and again still nothing. I went searching and nothing, there were no energy beings, nothing, just emptiness and stillness.

Then I was shown what I can best describe as a static lightening bolt, an elongated Z, like you may see in a cartoon. I just looked at it and nothing happened. Christine asked me to move closer and I did but still nothing happened. Then Christine asked me to touch it and when I did it was like getting a massive electric shock.

I was physically shaking and twitching like I was having a fit. It seemed to go on for ages, my arms and legs violently twitching and shaking. I was about to ask for it to stop as I felt I couldn't take anymore, when it subsided and then stopped.

Christine was as surprised as I was. She had never seen anything like it. Putting the footstool back in place, she restored the blanket over me and asked me to settle down and return to a calm state as she began to put me back in trance.

I settled down but before I could return to a trance state, I got another electric blast. The same thing again, shaking and violently twitching and this time a lot of laughing from my guides. They said, "You thought we'd stopped, well we tricked you but we have now." Again, it subsided and stopped.

Just as I resettled and for a third time, there was another blast and more hysterics on the other side. "Stopped now," they said, then another blast. "No we haven't", more laughter, so much laughter. They were having the time of their... um, spirits? I can hardly say 'lives'.

My guides found the whole thing hilarious but I felt they were laughing with me not at me as this was part of their big picture. Something to which all parties had agreed and they had some fun delivering it. Boy did they have some fun, seemingly at my expense but all I could do was laugh.

Then it did finally stop completely. It took a while for my body to settle and I had a number of tremors but these were at a relatively low intensity. My body was recovering and I settled down to slowly go back into trance.

Christine asked how much soul energy I was given. They said 15 per cent as my body couldn't handle any more than that. I would have to get more physically fit and stop drinking, at which point I laughed as much as they were, which is all they seemed to do. "Stop drinking?" I said incredulously. "Yes," they said.

Christine asked my guides what was I meant to be doing with my life. They said, "You're so obstinate; you already know." To which Christine replied, "Today is the first time I have met Dave and I don't know, please can you tell me?"

"He's a healer," they said. Christine asked if healing was one-to-one or one to many. "It is both, with more emphasis on teaching many", they said.

According to Christine, this regression was very unusual as people very rarely get an energy boost. She was aware of just two other occasions where it had happened in all the 12,000 regressions performed by MNI practitioners. I was the third.

When we finished I was a little dumbfounded as I didn't really understand what had happened but I did feel really good. I felt energised and vibrant as if I needed to go dancing. Christine wasn't prepared to let me leave until I'd convinced her I was sufficiently grounded to drive. We had a coffee and I pretended to Christine I'd calmed down but inwardly I was on the ceiling.

I now recognise how much that regression changed me. I explained to people at the time that it was like I'd been living my life in monochrome and now I was living in colour. A few weeks later, I lost the desire for alcohol. I just didn't fancy it at all and I stopped drinking with ease.

Past life regression (PLR)

After such a profound and incredible experience with Christine, I wondered what the PLR course would bring. What could be next that Nicola had seen?

There is much debate about PLR. Detractors say there are just too many people claiming to have been Napoleon, Caesar, Joan of Arc, Cleopatra, etc. for PLR to be real. Others have researched individual cases and found discrepancies in dates and events, which is something else that raises doubts about the veracity of past lives.

Quantum Physics and Buddhism for that matter say time is an illusion and hence how can we have previous lives it would seem a contradiction. However our three-dimensional experience is only a small element of what is actually going on.

Whether we connect to a 'collective consciousness' having the experience of the life we tune into, or whether we actually have had that particular life ourselves isn't really important and I'll explain why, but first I want to address the case of historical inaccuracy in past life regressions.

Most cases of historical inaccuracy do not consider the vast majority of detail that is correct. Consider your own memory; think about something long since past. How sure are you that you can recall all the details accurately?

The truth is, the detail is not important. What is important is the experience; what it means to the client, and how it is dealt with. As a therapy I know myself it is brilliant, it uncovers information we would never find through conventional methods.

Traditional hypnotherapy starts with the client discussing an issue through their conscious understanding. The therapist delves into the issue and looks for a cause and then creates a metaphor to address the unconscious mind.

PLR is the opposite way around. We ask the unconscious mind for the issue the client is facing. The unconscious mind provides the metaphor, which we can consider to be a past life. The PLR therapist then resolves that experience at the soul level. There is no deeper resolution.

If we approach PLR through traditional material science processes and look for flaws, we can find many. If we focus purely on the outcomes we find a wonderfully successful process, evidentially it works. In my view it works successfully because we are all living with baggage. If we remove the baggage from a 'previous life' then in this one it never existed. Our behaviours automatically change as we've become more congruent with self.

I've seen amazingly deep transformations through PLR and hence it is my favourite form of therapy.

Hogwarts

I travelled to Dorset for the course held in Gaunts House near Wimborne. Gaunts House is an old mansion where some very weird things went on, hence we affectionately called Gaunts House, 'Hogwarts'.

I was with 15 other delegates, Andy and two assistant tutors. Some very odd things happened and I miss the place and especially the people. I witnessed some absolutely fantastic transformations.

I'd explained to Andy why I was doing the course and that I'd only be doing the first module. Each module was four days and the full course was four modules with two months separating each.

At the beginning of the course I was little concerned as I witnessed people going through a full catharsis from reliving a highly charged physical and emotionally difficult death. In all my previous therapy training I'd been taught to keep the client out of the trauma. Here, we searched for trauma and relive it in it's full capacity. I wasn't sure this was for me. Then it was my turn.

I went to a past life as a member of the Knights Templar, a religious order founded in 1119. As a Templar, I was tortured to death, which explains my antipathy toward the Catholic Church and my long interest in the Templars. I released so much suppressed anger, shouting, kicking and punching. The death was not difficult to relive, as I didn't feel any pain. It was considerably worse to observe than to experience.

Following my death on the rack, I met the perpetrators in the soul world and they felt deeply sorry and it was easy to forgive.

Healing at this level is very powerful and I released a huge amount of negative emotions.

I learnt so much on the first module, the people were fantastic, the course so good and we had so much fun. Consequently I ended up doing all four modules. In each module I had at least two, three-hour regressions. There was a lot more in PLR than I'd appreciated, we covered a lot of ground.

There are two other regressions that I feel are significant albeit in reality they all were.

In another regression, I saw myself as a Roman in Greece, the son of a tyrannical governor although I'd grown up largely unaware of my father's cruel style of leadership. He died and I became the governor, it was my intent to release all the jailed elders and local leaders as a sign of good will. My advisors resisted though, they were adamant it would be a mistake and said it would cause a revolution. I was not convinced but delayed a decision.

I was taking a vacation on the coast with my wife, a beautiful Greek woman. I walked toward the sea and had the water at my feet when I heard a commotion from behind. I turned and saw fighting, the small platoon I had with me for protection was being overrun and my outnumbered soldiers were being killed.

At that moment an arrow struck me right in the middle of my chest and I fell backwards, thinking to myself, "what a good shot from that distance". I raised my head and saw my wife being taken away. She looked back at me and our eyes locked. I immediately recognised that it was Steph and I knew she had tipped off the local people as to our location. She had arranged my murder.

I wonder if this would be acceptable grounds for divorce two thousand years later?

At the soul level I discovered what my father had done and why on his death there was a sense of revolution. I met the locals and heard their stories of murder, rape and more. I was devastated that I hadn't known about this but I could have done if I'd followed my intuition and released the elders when I wanted to, possibly saving my own life at the same time.

The lesson for me there was very significant. Follow my intuition, do what I feel is right and not what others consider correct.

Another regression I feel is worth explaining was on the last module, some six months after my soul regression with Christine. Bryn Lewis was the therapist and I asked him for his account, he kindly provided the following, some of which I'd forgotten, however we both have it on MP3.

Bryn's account.

"I regressed Dave whilst at Gaunts House in 2013. The intent for the session was to visit a past life that would benefit Dave's higher learning. He quickly went into trance and entered a past life as a young man near a tavern. After exploring the life, it appears that Dave was a merchant of some kind and had been making deals with the tavern owner to supply ale.

"Something went wrong with the deal and he was attacked in the tavern and stabbed. Believing he was dead, his attackers dragged him into the woods and buried him alive. He then died and I asked him to go to the spirit realms, where we performed some body therapy on the area of the wounds, removed the knife and performed healing on that area.

"I don't know why but I felt there was something that seemed to be missing so I decided to return to the body at the point of death to further explore what had happened to

the body. I asked Dave what happened after leaving the body at the time of death, he stayed looking over the grave. When I asked what happened next, Dave said the tavern had changed colour, his grave was now overgrown and suddenly cars were driving nearby where before there were only horses. There was an element of confusion as time seemed to be moving on and on but Dave seemed to be stuck in this scene watching over the body.

"I asked Dave to scan the body in the ground and check to see if any soul energy was remaining. He said it was just bones that were left so we set an intention for a thorough scan looking for soul energy. It was at this point Dave noticed a bright light in the heart area. Before I even had chance to ask him to retrieve the soul energy the whole room seemed to change energetically. Dave took a deep intake of breath as his back arched. For myself watching this event as a witness I can only describe it as a 'meeting of a lost friend'. The sense of completeness was incredible.

"Dave then was able to leave the scene and move into the light of his own accord. We asked the perpetrators of his murder to step forward so we could ask why this was to happen and get a greater understanding of the event.

"What was incredible was the attitude of the perpetrators. They were happy to see Dave and said they had been waiting a long time for him. We established that this death was part of a soul contract and Dave had actually agreed to being killed as part of his soul learning. What wasn't expected was the trauma that being buried alive would cause a soul fragment to remain in the body and prevent it returning back to source.

"Forgiveness is everything and this was reached with the perpetrators very easily. We allowed them to go on with their own journeys knowing everything from this life was resolved.

What is amazing with past life regressions is linking the life to current life issues and illnesses. We are able to see repeating patterns in people's lives that can be transformed in just one session. With Dave's regression, it appeared that the reason for going back to this life was only to retrieve the soul fragment. This in itself had a major therapeutic effect, a great session to witness."

Bryn Lewis
Crick, Warwickshire

All I would add to Bryn's description is that when I saw the white glow in the heart area and I accepted it, I instantly felt the energy enter me. My back arched and I heard two chairs slide along the floor. Bryn and the observer Paula both moved backwards in their chairs.

The impact of this session left me very confused, not at what had happened, it was how I felt, totally confused and again unable to fully reconnect with the three-dimensional world. I was completely disorientated and felt very strange and very uncomfortable, my change in behaviour was also noticed by others.

Andy did some energy work on me and I went to bed at 7pm straight after dinner, which I couldn't eat. That night I had a raging temperature and thought I wouldn't be able to continue on the course. However at 7am my temperature was normal and I did continue although Andy was aware I wasn't engaged with what was going on.

That evening I again couldn't eat dinner and was back in bed at 7pm. Again my temperature went high and again at 7am it came down. That day I was still not engaged with the training, I still felt so disorientated.

Despite all the grounding I did, it took another couple of days for me to settle back into a more regular connection with the physical world.

I do not know what happened and can only surmise. I believe I had a significant increase in my soul energy. Whether it was a soul fragment, or a scene allowing me to receive more soul energy I do not know. It had taken me 40 years to accept my boulder but now, as soon as I recognised this soul fragment, I had no hesitation in accepting it immediately.

I hadn't been drinking alcohol for several months and had lost weight, I was fitter than I was six months earlier but this additional energy still took its toll on my body.

I didn't know it then but I had gone through what is often called a 'Spiritual Emergency'. This is when there has been such a change at an energy level the conscious mind is unable to cope.

Janet Treloar and Zak

Midway through the PLG course there was an annual weekend at Hogwarts when people who had previously attended the course got together for presentations, workshops and a generally a good time. People could discuss new techniques they had discovered and issues they were facing. It was a great weekend.

Janet Treloar is a PLG therapist and more. She gave a presentation on 'Inner Child Regression' and sought a volunteer on whom to demonstrate. There was some reticence among the numerous attendees; we all knew this would involve bearing ones soul and detailing childhood issues. After giving others the opportunity to volunteer and seeing that nobody was going to, I raised my hand.

As it turns out I had no idea of the issues I'd suppressed through my childhood. Much suppressed emotion, copious tears and thankfully much relief. Janet uncovered so much long forgotten, small detail and with it call came floods of emotion.

Afterwards I was so pleased I'd volunteered and the observers said it was a very emotional experience for them, some noticing similarities with their own childhood. Again I have the session on MP3 although I've not had the inclination to listen to it.

Janet also taught us an Inca energy management technique that she learnt from a shaman in South America. This again is powerful and once shown it seems so obvious, it's a method of quickly removing internal energies that are not serving us and I describe it in Part 3.

One evening I overheard Janet say she's a channel, so I asked her about it and she agreed to a demonstration. There were about a dozen of us all fascinated to get a first hand experience of a channel.

Janet told us about Zak, the name of the entity that she channels. He last incarnated in the 14th Century and had a Buddhist lineage. Janet explained she would go into a meditative state where she always went to the same field and sat under the same tree. When she was settled under the tree she would see Zak approach and she would leave her body and Zak would then replace her.

Janet settled and became still and we waited. It was probably three or four minutes of silence until her face twitched and then she began to smile. Then in a totally un-Janet like voice, pronounced, "good evening", followed by a chuckle and "it's nice to meet you all". Janet's eyes were always closed although her head moved as if to look at the person Zak was addressing.

For about an hour we took it in turns to ask a couple of questions each. Zak does not give simple answers. I could tell by the amazed expression on other people's faces how impressed everyone was at the detail Zak was providing about their lives, their homes and the problems they were facing. Zak gets the information by communicating with our guides and they do know lot about us. I asked a couple of questions that on reflection were a little pointless considering with whom I was speaking.

Janet had suggested an hour, saying Zak could go on all night and we'd have to be the ones to call time. So after the hour it was suggested we called a halt, thanked Zak and asked him to let Janet return.

It was then that Zak introduced the guides that I described earlier and I was filled with the feeling of love and joy. I immediately recognised what had happened to me a year and a half earlier after walking around Poynton Pool, the feeling of utter joy outside the chip shop. Our guides is where our intuition comes from, following our intuition is following our destined path.

Just before Zak left, he turned to me and said, "and we shall be talking again soon", then he was gone. A minute or so later Janet returned with no knowledge of what had been said. Janet explained she decided a long time ago it was better to keep her distance and not hear what is said. If she gets close to her body under the tree she can hear Zak.

There is no doubt that Zak is for real. Later that night I thought of all the things I could have asked him rather than what I did ask so decided to ask for a one-to-one session.

The following morning I asked Janet and she said yes but there were two others who had already asked the same question. She said two hours was as much as she could do in one sitting so we all got together and agreed 40 minutes each.

I had a list of questions but now, some years later, I realise again how mundane they were. I've since spoken to Zak on many occasions and I'm getting better at selecting the questions and how to ask them.

Returning to Dubai after the last module I felt so different, Nicola had been right, the soul regression and PLR course had indeed changed me.

There was now an understanding and acceptance that my marriage was over and that the words Steph had spoken nearly two years earlier, "I'm letting you go, I'm setting you free, you are better off without me", were so true.

Russell was also right in that it was an angelic communication. To hear it, I'd had to be in the right emotional state, or more accurately, emotionless state and that is just what my higher self provided. I'd finally moved from a Level 1 resistance and realised a Level 5 listening. My box had been to try and hang onto a marriage that had served its purpose.

I was now ready for the new beginning but this time the old ideas had gone. I also believed I'd gone though enough transformation for one lifetime. How wrong I was.

9 Kenya

In 2013, just before the Muslim Holy month of Ramadan, I had an impulse to contact a friend in Nakuru, Kenya. Within 48 hours I was there. I am continually learning to follow my intuition, although sometimes it takes me a while to recognise the reasons for the journeys it takes me on. I had no plans, no knowledge of Nakuru or what I would do for the month I'd booked.

My hostess was Farah, a British woman of Asian decent. Farah had worked for NGOs (Non-Government Organisations) in Africa and been heartedly disgusted by the corruption. Little to none of the money allocated for children got anywhere near them. So she decided to do something about it and set up her own orphanage.

Our Roots Kenya

I can personally vouch that 100 per cent of the funds Farah receives goes to the children she cares so passionately about.

I'd met Farah in 2007, on a train travelling from Manchester to London. There was just the two of us sat diagonally opposite each other at a four-seat table. Suddenly the train came to an unexpected stop mid station as someone had jumped off a bridge ahead.

We started to chat about the delay and I discovered Farah lived in Manchester and commuted to London to study for a law degree. She was having huge logistical and financial problems, working part time to support herself, she was about to give it all up.

I asked her about her ambitions and she explained it was to work with children for the United Nations. We chatted for around two hours about how she could organise her priorities and find a way to get on the path she most wanted to take. Farah had a cause and we ended up swapping email addresses.

Farah went on to gain a BA (Hons) Politics and Law; MA International Politics and Human Rights; MA Criminology with Human Rights. An amazing woman full of life, vitality and enthusiasm, she now works tirelessly for the underprivileged across Nakuru.

Years later she kindly said that our conversation on the train had changed her life. Little did I know the impact she was about to have on mine, all because she'd settled in Kenya and I went to see her on an impulse.

I fell in love with Africa. It is a beautiful place full of wonderful people, financial poverty coupled with an abundance of love. When I look at the abundance of wealth in the West, it seems we're at polar opposites.

Farah took me to an area called the 'London Slum'. Built on a rubbish dump, it is the biggest slum or shantytown in Nakuru and home to about 200,000 people who live in extreme poverty.

Called the 'urban poor', the slums of Kenya have risen up as a result of the numbers of people leaving the rural areas to find jobs in the major cities. How this began and the West's behaviour toward Africa is brilliantly documented in a book I read whilst there called *Silences in NGO Discourse - The Role and Future of NGOs in Africa* by Issa G. Shivji. The West has a lot to answer for.

What was truly amazing is the warmth of the children of the London Slum. They have no material assets, nothing. They played with sticks, old tyres and string. Unrolling an old cassette tape was hours of fun. Yet they were happy, smiling and giving.

Buddha said, "Desire is the cause of all suffering." In the West, we are taught to desire things. Marketers make us wonder how we ever survived without something or other and not having the latest gismo makes us inferior, it's materialism. We have taught Africa materialism and the result is the slums.

Children in the London Slum, Nakuru Kenya, they were imitating me with my camera.

Africa taught me still more although it wasn't until long after I left I understood just why I had to go to Africa and why Nakuru.

Farah's friends were very kind and generous and one family in particular, Sarat, Radhika and their wonderful mother Namita. I was entertained regularly, we had some very interesting conversations over many lovely dinners and I learnt a lot about the Sikh tradition.

Sarat took me to the Ol Pejeta Conservancy, we had a fabulous weekend and I saw all the big five, the Elephant, Rhino, Leopard, Lion and Cape Buffalo. I was within just a few meters of them all and in particular the wonderful, powerful and most graceful Leopard. What an animal, to be so close, seeing it in the wild, to say I really enjoyed it doesn't quite cut it. To be within a metre or two of three Leopards, to watch them stroll so gracefully through the undergrowth was such a beautiful sight.

Many months later Zak told me that the reason I had to go to Africa was to be near the Equator as it had an energetic impact on me. It was not one I was consciously aware off but an impact all the same and I needed it for my inner growth and development.

I didn't recognise any energy on the Equator, I certainly did at Naivasha and Nakuru National Parks, immense energy, truly wonderful places.

Naivasha has a quality about it that I find it difficult to describe. Yes it is a beautiful place with the lake, the trees, the hippos and birds. Everything seems so integrated, there is a calmness and somehow a gentle yet powerful energy. It is the subtle feel of nature more than the visual experience of it.

The same is true of Nakuru National Park where I went with a friend very early one morning. We set off on the tour at sunrise and what an awesome experience it was, we toured the lake in about five hours seeing some wonderful sights, the scenery and animals were fantastic and I took many photographs.

On returning to the administration centre my friend decided to depart. I chose to stay and go around again in the afternoon, so after lunch off we went. I had the same driver but now it was just the two of us and he suggested an alternative route rather than the standard one we had done in the morning. I agreed, with no idea whatsoever what I was letting myself in for.

After a couple of hours and just after passing a pride of lions we came to Makalia Falls where there was a ford across a small river. The driver was not paying attention as he drove off the ford crossing and we got stuck. It wasn't much of a drama, the water was only a few centimetres deep, but it was soon to became one.

There were a few other vehicles around and attempts were made to pull the Land Rover out of the river, sadly they all failed and the driver called on his radio for help. It'd be an hour so everyone departed, leaving the two of us alone. Now I know a Kenyan hour is the same as a Dubai hour and nothing like a UK hour so I wondered if I'd be back before nightfall. I sat on the riverbank pondering why the universe had brought me here to get stuck. Then I felt the bites and noticed a large number of big black ants all over my legs. I didn't stay there very long.

I then remembered the pride of lions we had just passed and the big sign at the administration building saying, "Do not get out of your vehicle, there are dangerous animals…". From being calm my thinking head started thinking things it shouldn't and I considered returning to the Land Rover and the driver agreed it was the safest place. I settled down in the back and went to sleep.

I was awoken by the movement of the vehicle and looked out to see the river level had risen, only slightly but I had an immediate sense of fear that something was wrong and that I should get out. Just as I was picking up my rucksack, water burst through the side of the Land Rover and I was suddenly up to my waist in very fast flowing water. I was in the middle of a flash flood.

I stepped out onto the offside running board where I met the driver. The water was now up to our chests and the riverbank considerably further away than it had been earlier. There was no way I could see of getting to dry land, the quiet had gone, the falls had become a rage, the noise tremendous and the river a torrent.

Just as the severity of our situation began to dawn, I saw a lady running away. I thought to myself, "where did she come from and what a great help she is running away", to discover minutes later she was actually a great help indeed as help is what she was running for.

We would have died other than by a 'coincidence' a Dutch ex marine was part of a group camping nearby. Of all the places in a 188 sq. kilometre park this group had just arrived to camp no more than 100 metres away, their timing was immaculate.

Within a few minutes around 20 people had gathered on the riverbank and the marine took control. An ice pick tied to some twine was thrown over to us and with hand signals I was told to pull it. I pulled an orange nylon rope about half a centimetre in diameter to the Land Rover and for the first time in my life once being a Boy Scout came in handy, I tied the rope to the roll cage with a clove hitch.

A few men wrapped the other end around a tree and pulled it as tight as a piano wire. The rope had to be very tight as it was so very close to the water.

The driver went first. He was in his early 20s and he nearly didn't make it. He was facing upstream and as soon as he left the Land Rover his feet were swept from under him, he became horizontal, face down and his weight pulled him under, I noticed how really strong the current was. Thankfully he got across but it was a real effort and hence I thought my chances were significantly less.

It was an interesting experience and I said to my guides, "it looks like I'll be having another meeting with you sooner than I expected".

This photograph is a still taken from a smartphone video sometime after the event, the water level lower. The first one I took but my camera was a loss as were two iPhones and an iPad.

I was very calm, remarkably calm in fact but didn't think my chances were high. I looked downstream to see if there was anything to grab hold of if I got swept away. I also made the mistake of not taking my rucksack off. I later realised that was what everyone was shouting at me but it didn't cross my mind. It was nearly a fatal error.

The water was still rising and now bursting over the top of the Land Rover that was now shifting and far from stable. I feared it would get turned over and washed away so I thought there was no point in waiting any longer.

I got under the rope so it was across my chest and under my arms, I faced downstream and I left the Land Rover. I was immediately horizontal but facing up, my rucksack though acted like a sail pulling me down. I started pulling myself across, it was very hard and so much harder than it would have looked and it seemed as if I was spending more time below the water than above it.

I was about two-thirds the way across and thought if I take one more mouthful of water I'll be gone. I also realised how pointless it was looking for something that I could grab hold of downstream, there would have been no way. As I rose above the water to see sunlight, I took another breath, as I did I heard this marine shouting obscenities at me. I felt it annoying as I was trying hard to survive but his attitude did give me the strength for another pull along the rope.

Then a human chain was formed and a hand appeared, it seemed to take me an age to get the courage to let go and grab the hand but when I did I was suddenly very firmly pulled out and ended up kneeling on the bank.

I looked up at all the faces around me and sputtered, "Thank-you." Many voices were telling me I shouldn't have worn my rucksack. Odd I placed so much value on its contents, my wallet and passport were all that survived and they could have been in my pocket.

I was taken to their camp and dried in front of a campfire. Someone gave me some dry clothes. I was then told the Land Rover had gone; later finding out it was totally submerged and invisible.

We were saved by a group of Dutch tourists who had just arrived and were setting up camp around a huge double decker safari coach. No one was allowed to leave camp until it was complete. One lady broke the rules. She wanted to see the Falls and was told to wait, it was dangerous to go alone. Once the camp was complete and they would all go together. She didn't, she went on her own and said she didn't know why she did it, she just felt compelled to. If she hadn't I doubt we'd have survived. Thankfully she was following her intuition, her gut feeling.

After a while a Kenyan Army vehicle arrived and I was taken back to my apartment and asked to return the following day to complete paperwork.

At around 9pm, I walked into the apartment I shared with three others. No one was there and I busied myself drying my phones in rice anticipating the shock to hit, which it did. I then found half a bottle of Bacardi and that didn't last long, it was really good therapy although I still had a restless night.

Returning the following day I saw this massive coach outside the administration block and the people that had saved our lives. I handed back the borrowed clothes and thanked them again and again. Really, what can you say? Thank you didn't seem sufficient.

The park manager enquired why I went around a second time and I explained how the park "felt" and he said, "You're not European; you're African. Europeans don't feel the parks they see them. Africans feel the parks."

Here in lies a difference with the West. We've lost the sense of feeling energetic places such as Stonehenge. We analyse the stones, we measure them but we don't feel them. We're into thinking and measuring not feeling or sensing. That's what our education system and culture has done for us, it's shut out our most important attribute.

I asked Zak what on earth I was meant to learn by such an event. He explained that my higher self had volunteered for someone else's learning as, he said, "you were best able to deal with it". I can see the wisdom in a military expression, 'do not volunteer for anything', and I've asked they don't do it again, but as I'm learning some things are just not in my control.

I learnt a lot in Kenya. I will always remember those wonderful children in Farah's orphanage and those in the London Slum. I am in awe of Farah who works tirelessly for others. If the world had more like her, it'd be a far better place.

This all started because someone jumped off a bridge. One can reflect and surmise that they were in despair. They would have a family and friends. One way or another it is a complex set of circumstances and events that we are all involved in. Actions we take can have massive consequences, most of which we may never discover.

10 Not a corporate ladder

I returned to Dubai only a few days after the Nairobi airport fire, the temporary terminal facilities were very good and the Makalia Falls incident was behind me.

Back in Dubai I had a story to tell and fortunately a lot of photographs as the camera memory card survived.

I was reading a lot and doing a little therapy. I didn't advertise myself and ended up working at a therapy centre. Initially this seemed a perfect fit, clients would be sourced and I didn't have to advertise or market myself. As time passed it wasn't working out as I had to source my own clients and the centre took 60 per cent, it didn't seem equitable, so I left.

I met others who ran therapy centres and although everything seemed to fit, I didn't feel I did. Externally, logically and rationally it fitted, internally I lacked the drive and enthusiasm, they just didn't feel right.

These false starts had me really wondering what it is I should be doing with my life. Even though I felt fine in myself, I had no motivation to continue with any of the work I found.

I knew motivation had to come from within but where was it? I felt like I was in no-mans land stuck between two things and I didn't know what either was or where they could be found. I asked Zak and he said everything was fine, there was no need to worry but I was worried and it was caused by the pressure of others saying, "You should be doing something." My thinking logical head agreed whilst my inner feeling was, "Just be, everything is fine."

I'd had this inner dialogue for sometime, the difference between 'doing' and 'being'. The former is our society's conditioning it starts early and never really stops until we retire, if we get that far. Being busy is a measure of success and I knew it to be false. I've been there and done that, it doesn't create happiness; in fact more often than not it creates the opposite.

Whereas living in the moment, mindfulness and meditation were 'being' and that feels so much better. So I was 'being' plenty and wondering how long it was going to take for me to find my motivation; what would fire up a desire to do something. I had no idea what it was but knew it had to be meaningful and to do with healing, so why wasn't I advertising myself and working as a healer?

Then out of the blue one of my clients asked to see me to discuss a business opportunity. He was a marketer something I'm not into and he explained how it was all to be done. I was easily convinced as I'd be training and I enjoyed helping people so I thought I'd give it a go.

Initially the motivation came freely, I produced a quantity of course material and I loved it. "Ha, this could be it!" I thought. I like writing and I like training. I had been a corporate trainer in British Telecom delivering strategic selling courses, this coupled with my commercial experience I could utilise without being inside that corporate box again. For weeks I was busy producing courses outlines that were more than one step above what I saw as the local competition.

However weeks turned into months and we hadn't done anything, no clients. There always seemed something else, waiting for something or for someone and always delays. I was becoming impatient.

It got to the point where I became frustrated and I recognised some old behaviour traits reappearing, I was again becoming a corporate manager and taking charge of the things I perceived were not being done. I lost my inner peace but thought it was just a stage I had to go through because at the end of this tunnel I'd be in front of and helping people, so it'd be worth it.

On Thursday 30 January 2014, I'd got the keys to my new apartment. I had furniture lined up for delivery on Saturday so my plan was to paint the living room on Friday. I wasn't in the best frame of mind that day, I was consumed with the frustrations with work and I was acting like a corporate manager again. However I was determined to enjoy painting the apartment, as I knew it would be therapeutic. I could put all this work business behind me to focus mindfully, on the job in hand.

I was going to do a wonderful job with a very pale green matt emulsion. The problem I identified was that the marble floors were very smooth and the ladder I'd bought had plastic feet, not a good combination. However it could work if I aligned the foot of the ladder with the ridge between the floor tiles.

I set it up and very carefully tested the ladder. Perfect.

It was on the third move of the ladder where something went wrong. As I got to the top of the ladder, the very top, the bottom started to slide along the tiles. I came hurtling down and hit the marble floor prone.

I smashed my face into the ladder breaking my right cheekbone. I broke my left wrist, smashed my right elbow and shoulder and dislocated my left big toe.

I got up but in no pain. There was paint all over the floor and the blood pouring from my face made quite a contrast. I couldn't move my right arm although somehow and for some strange reason, I put the lid on the paint can and had to use a hammer to seal it. How I managed that with a broken wrist I don't know, nor do I know why I bothered.

I called Sue. No answer. I waited a few minutes and called again, still no answer. So I sent a text, a single word. "Help." Sue had been in her garden and not heard her phone, however fortunately she went inside for something just as the text came in. She rang me and asked, "Are you all right?" "No," I said, nothing else, just the one word and the phone went dead.

Sue was round so quickly she must have broken every traffic law in the book. She took one look at me and got me straight to hospital where I stayed for 12 days. I was in the operating theatre for six hours. I have, according to my physiotherapist, more metalwork in my right arm than she had ever seen in one person. I'd avoided looking at the x-rays and took her word for it, then she swivelled the screen to show me, I wish she hadn't.

The surgeons used two plates to put me back together. One held my shoulder together and the other my elbow. Each plate had about a dozen screws that look more like nails. I'd really smashed myself and made a real mess. Both the surgeons, one specialising in shoulders, the other in elbows, did a marvellous job in rebuilding me. So well in fact that when I went back two months later for a review and more X-rays they were more interested in congratulating each other on their work than talking to me. Two very professional orthopaedic surgeons, I felt I was very lucky indeed.

They also told me I was lucky. If my head had taken the impact rather than my right arm and shoulder, I've have been brain damaged or died.

On the way to the hospital, Sue had been concerned I may pass out and was talking to me constantly. She asked, "Is there anything you need?" I replied, "Yes a large Scotch." Then I said, "Everything happens for a reason Sue and one day I'll look back at this and know it was for the best."

Little did I anticipate it would take less than five months to figure out the reason for the fall. Looking back now I'd change nothing as the fall set in motion a chain of events that could never have happened otherwise.

It was Wednesday 12 February when I was released from Dubai's Sheikh Rashid Hospital. Sue looked after me whilst I was convalescing, something for which I'll be eternally grateful. On the first evening, she presented me with a bottle of my favourite malt whisky, Glenmorangie. I hadn't drunk alcohol (other than in Kenya) for over a year and cannot deny I enjoyed it. Although looking back I wish I hadn't said what I did about wanting a whisky on the way to the hospital as alcohol once again became part of my diet.

During the initial stage of recuperation I had a lot of time on my hands. I couldn't do much. My left wrist was in a fibreglass splint and my right arm in a sling and I could barely move it. I read and spent a lot of time on the web. One of the videos I came across was Graham Hancock talking about Ayahuasca and consciousness; I was more than a little interested.

Zak again

I decided to ask Zak what was going on and set up a Skype call with Janet. Zak's response surprised me.

I asked Zak why I was so stupid to climb a ladder I knew to be unsafe. His answer was, "You were not stupid you were following guidance." This was difficult to understand and I questioned the legitimacy of such guidance.

In the conversation that followed it was taking Zak longer to respond than usual, and he told me that, "Your guides are being a bit bashful, if guides can be bashful." He felt he wasn't getting down to the reasons behind the fall. Then the call cut, I lost the Skype connection with Janet.

The following day Janet emailed me. Her PC died due to a power supply problem and when she got it going again the internet connection failed. She said this is very odd, as she doesn't believe in coincidences. Later she got a message from Zak saying not to reconnect with me for another two weeks. He needed to get to the bottom of the reason for the fall. This I did find odd as time doesn't exist on the other side and I still don't understand the delay.

Two weeks later I was back with Zak and was impatient to understand what had happened.

Zak explained that within my soul plan there was an exit point. It had been agreed before this incarnation that I could have an accident that would enable me to return home or - in three-dimensional language - die. It was to have been quick and painless. This was included in my soul plan as an option should Steph and I not have split up. Our parting was planned, one-way or another it would happen.

One of my guides, I'll call him 'Bashful', is my healing guide. Bashful felt I was moving too far 'off plan' by going corporate again and I needed pulling back.

Summarising a long conversation, Bashful and another healing guide, I wish I knew their names, went to my higher self and used the exit option in my 'Soul Plan' as leverage to change my direction and higher self obviously agreed. However Zak felt the guides had exceeded their authority and when he got involved, the guides knew it, hence they were reticent in explaining to him what happened. Zak said, "I'm the last one they wanted digging around this."

It seems there is a structure of some form up there. However as Zak explained, he had now involved himself with my guides and a new outcome had been agreed. From here on in everything was going to be fine, there was going to be a change in direction and that I needed to consider the future not as a new chapter in a book, more like a totally new book.

From here on there would be more "lustre" in my life, I would be meeting more high vibrational people and there will be a lot of change. Everything I may desire was there for me. I had no responsibilities to others, now I had only to consider myself.

He further explained that my guides have not incarnated for a very long time and may have just lost touch a little with what three-dimensional life was like.

It was a lot to take in and I've had to listen to the recording a few times to fully appreciate all that was said. Zak doesn't use five words when 20 will do but as time passes I recognise how clever he really is. It's not that he isn't specific, but he doesn't close doors or open them, well not directly.

I asked Zak about Ayahuasca, was it right for me? He said, "Very timely."

An interesting point here is that following the surgery I refused both morphine and intravenous paracetamol. Despite the significant trauma I had no pain other than when I was being manoeuvred for the initial x-rays and CT scans, that was very painful. The lack of pain following the surgery surprised the doctors and nurses and the physiotherapist I later saw.

The conversation with Zak explained a lot about the reason for the separation. It was me that should have left Steph. Her path is to learn to fend for herself and not rely on others. If we hadn't separated I'd have had an accident and been 'taken out'. So the courage she showed saved my life. What a complex web this 'life business' really is. It also explains something else.

I've seen Steph in many regressions; the reason I had to have an exit in my soul plan was because we are close at a soul level. The possibility that we wouldn't split up was anticipated. Steph showed she was ready to take on her soul purpose by doing what I couldn't.

This new understanding explained a lot but I still had no idea what lay in front of me, but as I've said before, looking back now

I'd change nothing. Everything happens for a reason and that reason is our own spiritual growth. It is nothing to do with money or material wealth or asset collection, nothing at all, nothing.

Confusion

After several conversations with Zak, I've learnt that what he says often takes a while to sink in. It's like I understand the surface things then a few days later a deeper understanding arises. The other side is not language driven, it's telepathic and energy driven and Zak has to interpret the energy into language that the person he is talking to will interpret correctly. This is not easy and I've noticed this when listening to other people's recordings with Zak, he seems different with everyone.

I had a lot to integrate. What did it all mean, this 'new book' and starting over? How did I translate that into what it was I'm meant to do now? The training prospect had disappeared as my now ex-partner wished to go it alone.

I had a trip back to England planned. It was our children's birthdays, the three of them occur within 13 days of each other so I decided to take a detour and include Ayahuasca in my itinerary.

I still had no motivation but was happy enough, however with the hospital bills and the furnishing of my apartment, my logical head was saying "do something", whilst my intuition was saying, "everything's fine".

I felt my destiny was planned. My guides' intervention when I was looking at returning to the commercial world was stark enough. I didn't need that lesson twice thank you very much. But just what was I meant to do? There had to be something driving this, an end point, otherwise I may as well have died in the fall. I was still very confused.

Zak's assurance that there was nothing to worry myself about and that everything was fine, was all well and good but my bank manager hasn't met Zak and I somehow doubt his assurance would carry much weight. However there were no immediate pressing financial issues, it was just that if I didn't do something to earn some money soon, there would likely be financial woes in the future.

My life was fine, I was meeting more people that not only understood me but were also keen to explore my experiences and share theirs. We'd set up a discussion and meditation group, for people looking at me my life may seem pretty damn perfect.

One morning I was alone in the pool, just having done my physiotherapy, my arm was getting a lot better, it was about 9am and the water was beautiful. I looked around and thought to myself, 'just be and appreciate what you have right now. No worries other than those you choose to give yourself'. Then my thinking mind jumps in and says, 'this cannot go on forever you idiot, you have to do something'. The internal dialogue kicked off again but I could put it away and I did.

Ayahuasca was looming then I was off to the UK to see family for birthdays so, what the hell, nothing was going to happen before I leave, so just 'be' for a while.

So I did, I just lived more in the moment more than I had for sometime. I had some fascinating conversations with high vibrational people and I thoroughly enjoyed coffee shops and evening dinner discussions.

I'd put off anything concerning "doing", I was properly "being" without the inner dialogue. This brought with it a real sense of comfort and wellbeing.

11 Ayahuasca and Stonehenge

I discovered Ayahuasca through watching a banned TEDTalk by the British writer and journalist Graham Hancock. I doubt I'd have watched the talk if it hadn't been banned.

Graham Hancock - The War on Consciousness BANNED TED TALK (18 minutes)

In this video, Hancock discusses achieving a heightened state of consciousness with plant medicines, in particular with Ayahuasca.

Hancock argues that psychedelics like Ayahuasca are a gateway to a whole new level of human consciousness. A consciousness that would collapse the current model valued by our society, which Hancock calls the "alert problem-solving state of consciousness".

This model, says Hancock, is woefully broken and in need of urgent replacement if we are to halt the environmental destruction, wars and famine that plague our planet. Hancock says that the cause of all our troubles is our disconnection from spirit. We must reconnect with spirit if we are to find a new direction and he argues that plant medicine like Ayahuasca brings about this reconnection.

Sounds like a wonderful thing to do doesn't it? It is but before you go booking flights to Peru, I must stress that Ayahuasca is a potent substance. Its effects, in my experience, are permanent. You cannot step back, it is a one-way ticket and definitely not for all. Indeed it is not a something I would recommend unless you are ready and knowing you are ready is when the plant calls to you. You sense this through intuition. If Ayahuasca is something you feel you want to do, then fine. If not, leave it.

After watching Hancock's video I felt compelled to take the journey and with Zak's confirmation that it was "very timely" for me, I felt the time was right. I was ready.

Within just a few days I'd found someone with whom I could take the Ayahuasca ceremony, how things can fall in place when they need to.

I met Erik on Skype. We discussed some of my experiences, my meditation practice and the reason for wanting to do it. Then we agreed a date and I got my instructions on how to prepare for the ceremony. These included no prescription medications for three days before and a strictly controlled minimal diet leading up to fasting for the final 24 hours.

I left Dubai with high expectations fully aware again that I really should have no expectations at all, just go with it, but I was still excited.

Erik is a really nice, warm-hearted guy with a wonderfully light energy, someone with whom it was easy to feel relaxed. We discussed the ceremony and process. Erik is not a shaman, he explained he'd be nearby if needed but he'd not otherwise interfere with my experience.

First meditation and intention setting. My intent was to learn, to understand more about the nature of the universe, to learn more methods of healing and heal my shoulder and elbow. There were candles and incense burning, I felt very peaceful and ready.

My journey lasted about 10 hours but it didn't start well. The first period, which I'm guessing lasted around an hour, was not pleasant. I even thought to myself that I'd made a huge mistake, as it would be insufferable spending another nine hours like the first.

Everything was dark, in more than colour and I had a most unpleasant feelings. There were serpents, evil looking dark serpents twirling around and around, many of them. It was very dark indeed; I began to feel very cold, as if the cold was emanating from the inside. The whole thing was very unpleasant. Erik was speaking to me, telling me to let go.

Apparently I needed to let go of the fear and allow myself to experience what I was being shown. I'd always thought I could 'let go' easily enough but now it proved more complicated than it sounded. I was being shown existence from the 'dark side' from a different perspective and I found it most uncomfortable. I had the perception that darkness was the opposite of light and light was good, so dark was bad. This caused a resistance to the dark based on this perception and it was something I had to release. When I finally did that and accepted dark as purely perception, we moved on and I warmed up.

Vibration was my next lesson. I heard and sang a vibrational range going from as high as I could sing, dropping through the range down into the deepest level that seemed to go below the 'Om'. We went up and down and always down to the Om where there was more darkness below. Finally I decided to go deeper and when I did the scale below opened up. The next time I went high a door opened and above there seemed a spiral to infinity and when I went down the same thing, a spiral going down and I was in the middle, the connection. This is what we are in the three-dimensional form. Once I understood this, we again moved on.

I was shown that pain is vibration and vibration can be used to heal and how to do it by associating vibration with the pain. This was something I'd learnt at the Buddhist Society, but only to address tinnitus, by matching the tone in the ear with one made by humming, tinnitus can be cured. I hadn't appreciated this technique could work with the whole body. As soon as the recognition dawned, we again moved on.

Our names identify us by vibration. I was known as Dave, it has a different vibration to the name I was being shown, by a visual representation of waves not with sound. I was shown the waves of David visually and was being told to call myself David. David had a more complete vibration. I accepted myself as David and sang the name looking at the complex vibrational qualities in both waves and colours. There are so many ways of saying the word and each had a totally different visual representation that depends solely on expression. This is where the meaning is expressed. Once I understood we again moved on.

I was then introduced to an alter ego that I later recognised was part of me some 30 years earlier. This part had been suppressed over the years of my marriage and now it came back very strongly. I became very vocal, talking to this other 'personality'. It was a long conversation about the state of Western society.

My alter ego decided to change the world and have it full of things only 'he' liked. Only to immediately recognise how boring that was and put things back just the way they were. His language was explicit, he called Erik a "fuckin' smart arse". He was coming out with all sorts of observational humour and I found the whole thing extremely entertaining, as did Erik who said he'd never had anyone so entertaining. That alter ego has now integrated within me, it was the 'id' missing from 'Dav(e)'. As soon as I recognised this alter ego was elements of myself that I'd suppressed over the past 30 years, we again changed scenes.

I was shown Sacred Geometry and how everything is created by vibration that seemed to have resonant nodes that create form. There was a massive human body, huge, at about 3 metres tall, all made of geometric shapes and the geometry seemed so beautiful.

The whole experience was an organised progression, like a structured presentation, taking me through different experiences. I'd stay somewhere until I understood what I was being shown and as soon as I had the recognition, we moved on to something else.

When I saw the huge body and the geometric shapes that created form I wanted to go into it as I felt I'd be able to repair my shoulder and elbow, but as much as I wanted to move towards it, I was pulled in another direction, and what a direction it was.

About half a dozen of the most beautiful naked women, inviting me to experience the pleasure of sex within rhythms and vibrations enhancing the experience, my immediately understanding was tantric sex although I wish I hadn't understood that quite as quickly as I did as again I immediately moved on.

Next stop was a massive evolving and spiralling toroid. It was beautiful, displaying rich vibrating colours with so much fascinating detail. I focused on trying to understand how its rotating and spiralling mass was moving but I couldn't, it was far too complex. At the centre of this fantastic form there was a Ram's head that I felt was so out of place.

I cannot describe the experience, I cannot express what this toroid was like it was awesome. It was beautiful, colour rich, bright and golden, it also had reds, greens and blues. So bright and with such vivid contrasts, many black lines forming Fibonacci spirals going around this rotating mass. I knew it was everything there is; it was perfect in every way. It cannot be anything else other than perfection; creation is perfection.

This toroid is the centre of creation, I wasn't told, didn't think about it, it was obvious, I just seemed to know it and as soon as I recognised that thought, we moved on.

Back to beautiful rhythmic chants, going through the scales, the higher the lighter, the lower the darker, this must have gone on for well over an hour, up and down the scales. I found it liberating, it was a beautiful experience of vibrational sound. I was taught some chants and now when I use them they seem to send me back, but sadly not all the way. I should probably do them more.

The chanting then took me to what I felt was the 'journey home', a gateway to ultimate love and I thought, 'how nice' but it seemed always out of reach, I wasn't allowed to go there and returned to the acknowledgement of vibration. Simple words and phrases seemed so rich in form.

Just after the original dark experience had ended I asked Erik what time it was, he said "do you really want to know?" That's why I called him a 'fuckin' smartarse'. Now I sang 'do you really want to know' for ages. There are so many ways it could be delivered and each had visually different shapes and colours, it was fascinating, I was totally lost in the experience.

All these different vibrations bring different meaning. Words don't carry meaning, it's the vibration behind them that does.

As the experience subsided, I went outside and the appreciation of nature was so different to that I had previously observed. The grass, trees, everything has a deeper sense of natural beauty and harmony.

The grass seemed unified, not as a field, but as grass, being as one. A bit like us, seeing ourselves as individuals but part of something much greater.

Some months later, I felt that the conscious recognition of what I was being shown was only a fraction of the learning and changes within my being that Mother Ayahuasca created. This shift was much more than the few degrees my boulder made some 14 years earlier. I was placed more firmly on the route I was to travel. I knew Mother Ayahuasca was a highly intelligent energy with wisdom beyond our understanding.

We know through Quantum Science that everything is energy vibrating and I was shown this in the most deep and profound manner. Our given names identify us and for me it was important to recognise the difference between Dave and David.

Albert Mehrabian, the Professor Emeritus at ULCA is right, how we say things carries the meaning not the words.

Bashar is a channelled entity similar to Zak, he is channelled by Darryl Anka. Bashar has a wonderful description of Ayahuasca and what it does. From my experience he is exactly right.

<u>Bashar - Ayahuasca</u> (6 minutes)

In this video Bashar explains that plant medicines take you into higher realms of consciousness to enable the experience of different dimensions. He also states the plants cannot mislead you however those experiencing the plants have their own filters and interpretations that can and do mislead people. That's the baggage we all carry and that must dispense with if we are to lift our vibration and experience the higher realms of consciousness.

Stonehenge

After Ayahuasca I returned to England to see my family and followed an intuitive feeling to go to Stonehenge before my return to Dubai. I had a rather long internal dialogue with myself about Stonehenge, there was no logical reason to go.

When I drove into the car park I was still in this internal debate, I wondered why I was there, my logical mind was saying, 'You've been before, why again?' I felt somehow compelled and I was struggling with my thinking mind questioning me constantly. Indeed the thinking head would just not let this one go, its intensity stronger than ever.

It was a typical April day in England, raining. I walked around the stones still wondering what on earth had brought me there; the internal dialogue stopped me from appreciating the energy of the stones. This and the weather seemed to put a resistive barrier around me and I had my own little black cloud to supplement the grey ones overhead. Something had brought me and I didn't know what it was, it certainly wasn't the stones.

I decided to leave so I got the bus back to the administrative centre and was walking toward the car park when I felt an urge to go into the museum.

I'm not particularly impressed with the English Heritage approach to Stonehenge. To me they have missed the point by miles. They focus on the archaeology, I've 'felt' the stones and there is energy about the site that is different. I hadn't though felt it on this occasion, my mood and own little black cloud had dampened me more than the rain.

The museum held little interest so I hesitated for a moment but then just found myself walking in.

I was half-heartedly watching a large visual display of the timeline when I found myself stood next to an English Heritage guide. I asked him why there was nothing about the energy of the site because I thought that was the point of it. He said it was English Heritage who controlled things and they are not into the more esoteric explanations. It was an obvious response and we parted.

I decided to leave, still wondering why I was there in the first place. Then the guide came back to me and said, "The site shaman has just arrived, would you like to meet her?" Suddenly all seemed apparent. I hadn't realised how tense I'd become until that moment when hearing that message made me relax and I felt a reassuring calm spread through me, my cloud made way for sunshine. We walked slowly towards a seated lady wearing a cloak and holding a wooden staff, she had a small garland of flowers in her hair.

The next two hours were fascinating. Siobhan, the shaman of Stonehenge, is very knowledgeable and explained so much about the stones and the site that I had never heard before. I hadn't appreciated the purpose and as I've had time to ponder what Siobhan said it's all made perfect sense, albeit it's not on the radar of English Heritage. I must point out the Siobhan is the 'unofficial' shaman, she is not recognised at the organisational level but is certainly recognised by the staff at a local one.

Siobhan explained that Stonehenge is actually an earth energy point that controls three differing dimensions. The interpretation I bring to her description would be three differing octaves of vibration that we on this planet experience. Put in simple terms Siobhan said these dimensions are;

1. Redemption; for those that see,
2. Chaos; those that refuse to see,
3. Madness; for those still battling with ego.

Without getting too hung up on terminology, having three differing dimensions of vibration running concurrently on our planet is easy enough to understand. We tune into and recognise what we resonate with. Living in the higher vibrational dimension we resonate or align with things only others in the same spectrum do.

Initially I'd considered the three octaves as a serial progression, what I interpreted from Siobhan was these three dimensions run in parallel, concurrently. This is how we find such different attitudes to spirituality.

We find the greatest egos, those that cannot be wrong, in the lower spectrum of 'Madness', those in their Level 1 box in their world of ego. When we look at the state of the world today, the wars, hatred, desire to control, the unequal distribution of wealth, living in negativity, destroying others, etc. It is sheer madness. Those in control of society are certainly not higher vibrational beings.

Then we have those in the middle who are living in Chaos. These are people who may appreciate what this book is about but feel trapped by conditioning and keep their heads down, closing their eyes to what is around them. According to Siobhan, they are "those that refuse to see" and who will tell themselves, there is no alternative. For them, there is no alternative until they make the conscious decision to open their eyes and create for themselves something different.

The higher vibrational beings that are listening and responding to their intuition and feelings are in Redemption. I interpret this as being the state where you don't need to incarnate again. It is a chance to move into the higher realms of consciousness; into a higher dimension permanently.

Siobhan's terminology may be different to mine but when she was telling me about the stones and the three differing dimensions there was an automatic inner acceptance, my feelings were, 'this is truth'.

After Siobhan had spoken she turned her attention to me, saying, "something has brought you here, what is it?" I didn't know but thought it must have been the explanation of Stonehenge. I briefly explained some of my experiences and the most recent one with Ayahuasca and how I just turned up.

Siobhan then asked me to hold her staff, telling me it dates back to the 14th Century. She asked me to point it north, I rotated the staff so the head pointed north and Siobhan asked me what I felt. "Nothing," I said. "So point it east," she said. Again I felt nothing, south and west were the same. Each time Siobhan asked me what I felt and I didn't feel anything other than disappointment that I hadn't recognised anything whatsoever.

Then she said, "Ask Gaia what it is you need." So I did. Wow, the impact of a simple question.

I felt as if the ground below my feet just opened up and a hole had appeared that spiralled down to the centre of the earth. I felt drawn down; a tingle ran down my spine, I felt connected to the centre of the earth. It only lasted a few seconds and I recall my head rocking backwards as I felt slightly dizzy.

Siobhan smiled and said "I knew there was something". I looked at her and asked, "what happened?" although I really should have figured it out.
"You were grounded," she replied.

It was at that moment I recognised the staff. At the top was a Ram's head. It was identical to what I'd seen at the centre of that giant rotating toroid during my Ayahuasca experience.

A few days earlier, I'd gone deep into the darkness and wasn't at all resistant. I knew how to ground myself but this was different. This was the mother of all groundings, I saw and felt it, it was so deep. I pondered on this for many months, why was it needed? I don't doubt for a second it was but for what purpose? I got the answer some 18 months later whilst meditating next to the Sacred River in Peru.

The two events, Ayahuasca and Stonehenge were linked, distance and time separated but what are they other than an illusion. I also believe this is what Kenya was about, grounding at the equator, connecting to earth energy. I was aware of spiritual experiences upstairs but I had been blind to the need to keep connected to the vibrations that create form, vibrations that manifest, which are those of mother earth, Gaia.

I can visit the guides and Gaia, we are one represented through a 3D experience. Vibration forms an illusion of separation, it's just the same thing, differently presented.

We are multi-dimensional beings, the link that creates our three-dimensional experience. We're doing this, all of us. Many before me have said it, and I thought I understood, but I didn't know. Once we get it, once we know it, things change.

Again a subtle change and a different feeling, it's subtle but different. I feel more whole and complete. There is no way of knowing when there is something missing. We believe ourselves to be whole but I learnt spiritually through the soul regression and the work Bryn did with me, there were bits missing.

I think of this like a bubble. Our awareness is the volume of our bubble; what's on the inside is what we know. As we learn more we add to it, our bubble expands and our awareness increases proportionally. Outside of the bubble is what we don't know. If we consider this 'not knowing' as the circumference of the bubble, then the outside is what we don't know. The bigger the bubble, the more aware we become of how little we know.

The smaller the bubble, the smaller the circumference, and the less we don't know, hence the more we perceive we do. Those who have a small bubble are not spiritually aware, yet they are so sure they know so much.

We are here to learn and grow. It wasn't until I understood the individual lessons Mother Ayahuasca was showing me did I move on. When I didn't fully get it fully the first time, I was shown a different way. The only way to learn about spirituality is through the experience of it. Forgiving and seeing our conditioning for what it is will increase the size of our bubbles.

Over the last five years if I'd gone back to the business world, or even got myself tied up with one-to-one healing, then I'd not have given the focus and attention to the things I did. I'd not have asked the questions, read as much, or found alternative views like those of Graham Hancock. When I did let my thinking head lead and I listened to others telling me that I needed to 'do' something, then spirit acted to get me back on track.

The link between the vibrational message from Mother Ayahuasca and the grounding by Gaia couldn't be anything other than planned, organised, set-up, predestined, to enable the experience.

Zak had been right, Ayahuasca had been very timely indeed.

Ayahuasca and psychedelic medicines

In the UK, DMT or Dimethyltryptamine is a Class A, Schedule 1 drug. It is also the active ingredient in Ayahuasca. It is illegal to possess, supply or prescribe. Possession of Class A drugs carries a maximum sentence of seven years' imprisonment and a fine.

Possession with intent to supply, trafficking offences and production of Class A drugs carry a maximum sentence of life imprisonment and a fine.

Pretty heavy for a substance that naturally occurs in the body. It is a natural plant medicine that has been used by the indigenous tribes of South America for centuries. Used for centuries without harm and indeed with tremendous beneficial therapeutic effects so why is it illegal?

Professor David John Nutt, DM FRCP FRCPsych FMedSci, is a British psychiatrist and neuro-psychopharmacologist specialising in research on recreational drugs. Nutt was once a UK Government advisor on drugs. He was fired following publication in *The Lancet* of a detailed study on the relative harm of recreational drugs.

His study is very interesting and the chart provides a summary of his findings.

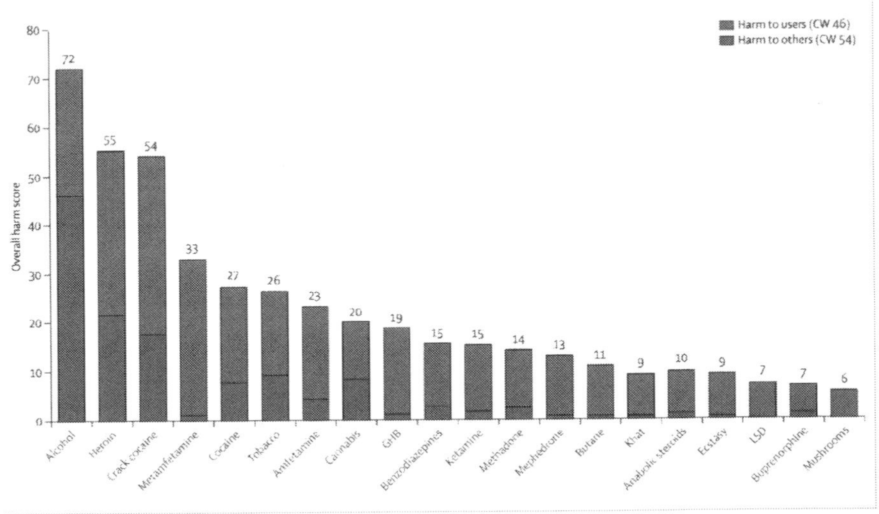

From left to right the chart reads; Alcohol (72), Heroin (55), Crack Cocaine (54), Metamfetamine (33), Cocaine (27), Tobacco (26), Amphetamine (23), Cannabis (20), GHB (19), Benzodiazepines (15), Katamine (15), Methadone (14), Mephadrone (13), Butane (11), Khat (9), Anabolic Steroids (10), Ecstasy (9), LSD (7), Buprenorphine (7), Mushrooms (6).

Nutt's detailed study found alcohol to be by far the most dangerous of all recreational drugs and tobacco to be the sixth most dangerous when both harm to self and harm to others are the measurement criteria.

The safest, by far, is Magic Mushrooms (psilocybin) and only slightly behind that is LSD and Ecstasy. Ayahuasca was not part of the study nor was Mescaline (Wachuma / San Pedro).
In this very interesting and informative video Nutt explains how propaganda is used to alienate the public about such things as Ecstasy.

<u>Prof David Nutt: Putting Neuroscience at the Centre of Drug Policy</u> (54 minutes)

If psilocybin is twelve times safer than alcohol, just why is the government so scared of its use to classify it as a Schedule 1 drug? The supply of which carries a maximum sentence of life imprisonment, the same as for murder. It just doesn't add up.

Ayahuasca, Wachuma and Magic Mushrooms open our minds.
They release us from the bonds of our Western-conditioned,
thinking clever heads and open us to the intelligence and
wisdom of nature, of the universe.

Alcohol, on the other hand suppresses. It is harmful and causes
so many direct and indirect deaths. I've enjoyed a glass or two of
red wine so I'm not advocating a ban on alcohol but I am saying
that banning psychedelics has no scientific or health justification.
Perhaps if more people took psychedelics and as a result became
higher vibrational, more intelligent and wiser, then maintaining
control by fear would become more difficult.

Was Professor Nutt fired because the last thing the government
want is a more intelligent and wiser society? A society based on
love, compassion and forgiveness and not material greed.

The banned TEDTalk by Graham Hancock that introduced me to
Ayahuasca is entitled *War on Consciousness*. There are a lot of

powerful vested interests in banning psychedelics and maintaining the status quo.

Wachuma (mescaline) is being successfully used to treat Post Traumatic Stress Disorder (PTSD), depression and stress. Magic Mushrooms (psilocybin) has been found to be a neurogenic regenerator. Research on these medicines is limited to countries where it is legal. The only people to benefit from their ban are pharmaceutical companies and those who wish to control others.

The Multidisciplinary Association for Psychedelic Studies (MAPS) is just one of many research institutes now focusing on psychedelics. For those interested their website makes interesting reading.

www.maps.org

Another interesting website is the Psychedelic Times, there is a lot of information about the health benefits of plant medicines and the research being undertaken.

Psychedelic Times

Dark Experiences and the misuse of Ayahuasca

One of the arguments I have heard against Ayahuasca is the potential for a so-called 'dark experience'. I was taught how to treat someone who has had a 'bad trip' on my PLR course. There are definitely those who do have a dark experience and fail to integrate or understand what it was that Ayahuasca showed them.

I've had a number of dark experiences with both Ayahuasca and Wachuma. I have also counselled people who have had dark experiences. I believe them to be the greatest of all learning opportunities. They offer the opportunity to take the largest single step forward in personal development, although it may not always be visible to the conscious mind.

In very simple terms, a dark experience is shown for a reason. I believe it needs to be understood not rejected. The plant medicines cut through so much to show you what is needed. A dark experience is something from the past that is simply lacking love. Forgiving self and acceptance that it is part of self is so important. The solution is offering love and compassion, acceptance and forgiveness. The darkness dissipates, allowing the experience to unfold.

Ayahuasca has become a popular experiment for many seeking enlightenment from the Western paradigm. It has become a business in many parts of South America with many jumping on the bandwagon. There are some serving the medicine that call themselves shaman and add another plant medicine such as Toê.

Toê certainly increases the psychedelic experience but extreme care needs to be taken when dealing with Toê. Too much can have serious detrimental effects. It is my belief that, those who suffer psychological issues after taking Ayahuasca, may have been given too much Toê.

Ayahuasca is safe. Adding a very small quantity of Toê is safe but adding too much is dangerous.

Another element of Ayahuasca is that whilst in the experience, people are vulnerable, especially women. There are a few people who call themselves shaman but who take advantage of women during an Ayahuasca experience.

People travelling to South America for an Ayahuasca or Wachuma experience need to take care and research with whom they are entrusting themselves.

The above is the dark side. For the vast majority, Ayahuasca and Wachuma offer an experience beyond their wildest dreams.

12 Standing Outside Time Itself

We've all seen science fiction movies that involve time travel. I grew up with Dr Who, a British science fiction TV show depicting the adventures of a space and time-travelling alien called 'The Doctor', it's now a cult favourite. It was an amazing concept for that 'time'. There have been many other authors and scientists that have contemplated the meaning and measurement of this concept we call 'time'.

Generally, we conceive time as a linear progression like a line, history to the left and the future to the right. Time travel just means jumping out of the now and jumping back in again at a different location. Within NLP, there is a therapy known as TimeLine where that is exactly what is done.

Science debates if time travel is possible this involves all sorts of scenarios involving wormholes and other complex theories.

However let's look at this from a totally different perspective. Buddhism says that time is an illusion and Quantum Scientists agree. However how on earth can we accept that time does not, in reality, exist. This is totally counter intuitive it goes against everything we know and understand. We've all had a childhood we all have a history. Everyone knows about WWII we all know it happened. If there's no such thing as time, where was I yesterday and how am I getting older?

The idea that time is an illusion, something that does not really exist, seems so bizarre that even to consider it seems a waste of time. But let's imagine what would exist if time didn't. What would we have if we didn't have time?

Time separates events so without it everything would happen simultaneously, at the same 'time'. Everything would co-exist. This includes all the events of yesterday and of tomorrow, of last and next month, last year, next year, etc. Seem odd? Can we get our heads around this or is it a perfect example of 'Cognitive Dissonance?'

I've had the experience now four times that time is an illusion and that everything does co-exist. This discovery though was one of the most frightening things I have ever experienced.

After Ayahuasca and Stonehenge, I returned to Dubai I felt different and everything seemed different. I was no longer seeing things, seeing my reality from the same perspective. Those who know me well commented that I was somehow a little different but they couldn't put their finger on what it was. To say I was more settled would suggest I was less settled before and maybe I was.

I noticed my meditation was different, it was somehow easier, I'd settle quicker and felt I was going deeper. I also had more preference for solitude. I no longer had music on in my apartment, preferring silence and I cancelled my TV subscription package. Although I did keep the sports channels so my TV wasn't totally redundant. So there were these subtle changes and I wondered what they would bring. I noticed I was in a space of 'surrender to' rather than 'going to get'; I was more going with the flow of life.

I settled back into a nice daily routine and restarted my physiotherapy in the pool. Fortunately the lack of it whilst I was away didn't seem to have any detrimental effect. I meditated daily and met with friends at my favourite coffee shop, JamaicaBlue. The discussions we had revolved around consciousness, dimensions and the degree of pre-destiny in our lives that leads to the question, how much are we really in control?

I also noticed a difference in my friends. It was not that they had changed, it was that I saw them from a new perspective. I was more sensitised to the vibration of their words and sensed their congruence differently. I felt more sensitive to other people's energy, sensing their inner state and in some the non-congruence with how they like to project themselves. I seemed to have a heightened sensitivity to one person in particular, my housemaid.

The maid came once a week for three hours and as soon as I saw her again, I felt something was wrong. I was very uncomfortable in her company, which was unusual because I'd known her for a long time. She had been working for my friend Sue and I'd asked her to come and work for me as I liked her. However now when she spoke to me I felt total incongruence in her words and I couldn't even look at her in the face, I couldn't hold eye contact. I spent quite sometime meditating on this trying to find the reason, however nothing was forthcoming.

After a couple of weeks and for some reason, I counted the money in my wallet and there were six 100 dirham notes. My wallet was then put in my rucksack, which I zipped up and left hanging on the back of the dining room chair while I went down to the pool.

On my return, I went to the mall to do some shopping. When I came to pay I noticed I only had only five 100 dirham notes. I thought long and hard, could I have made a mistake?

The following week I not only counted the money but also took all the serial numbers of the notes. I left my apartment at 9am returned at 10.30am. A 100 dirham note was missing and there had been only one person in the apartment other than me. My heart sank. The housemaid never returned. I decided that the cleaning and ironing was very good physiotherapy and a good way of practicing mindfulness. So it may seem every cloud does have a silver lining.

During one of the discussions in the coffee shop, with my friend Owen and we were getting deep about the nature of reality and consciousness, when an out-of-the-blue memory emerged. It had absolutely nothing to do with what we were talking about, it just popped up like these things do. So I explained to Owen something most odd that had happened about 15 years earlier, something I had completely forgotten until this conversation jogged my memory.

It had been in 1998 during the bidding of GCHQ, in the early stages when the team was working out the Group 4 Headquarters in Broadway, Worcestershire. Major bids are long processes and the early stages are considerably less stressful than the latter ones. The team was relatively small at around half a dozen and I had decided on the strategy for our element of the bid. It would be fair to say I felt pretty settled. I had confidence in the team, a unique and very cost efficient proposition that addressed some long-term client risk issues.

I was sat at my desk with the dawning realisation that I was losing the plot. I couldn't determine if a meeting I had yesterday, was one planned for tomorrow. This was so strange, but I seemed to know the outcome without knowing if it had taken place. The logical mind says, if you knew the outcome it had obviously taken place, but I didn't know if it had. Was I was projecting my thoughts as to the outcome I wanted? This only partly describes the confusion that seemed to spread through me very quickly. Within a few minutes I felt very disorientated.

My daybook didn't provide any answers, just more confusion as I confirmed the things that hadn't yet happened, but those things that had happened seemed to present further confusion because all they seem to provide was countless other possibilities.

This was nothing like being psychic, more the loss of understanding or recognising days and hours, time itself. It was as if I was outside time floating above it where I could only observe. I had no idea where those around me, or the circumstances I was in, fitted within a linear concept. I couldn't identify the difference between past and future.

I became very unsettled indeed thinking there was something very seriously wrong. I left the office and went back to my hotel and turned my phone off. Lying on the bed I tried desperately to focus and bring things back to normality but it didn't work.

I did not know if the events of the previous day had happened, or if it was my imagination giving me a scenario that I favoured for a meeting tomorrow. Even leaving the office half an hour earlier confused me. Had I had breakfast, am I going to the office or have I been, should I go now? I studied my watch it gave me focus. A few seconds later I didn't know if I'd studied it or I was thinking what a good idea it would be. This was living in the moment only and it was terrifying, I thought I was losing my mind completely, going mad.

How can I hold a conversation? I lay on my bed hoping everything would come back. Everything was jumbled up, yesterday, today and tomorrow were all the same, I couldn't separate them.

I decided to go back to the office and just be part of what was going on hoping this would provide the grounding I felt I needed. When I arrived, my number two Dave Parkin greeted me with the usual barrage of questions. I didn't answer a single one, made an excuse about a headache and sat down. For the rest of that day and the following one I said next to nothing. I sat in meetings without daring to open my mouth with fear I'd say something totally stupid. This was a real change of behaviour and it didn't go unnoticed. How I got through it I do not know.

Then everything came back, it was in the morning over breakfast that I realised what day it was, odd as it may sound, I hadn't known for the previous two. Everything started fitting in place and I was so relived.

It was around 10am that morning that unannounced my boss, Dave Keegan, arrived. I usually spoke to Dave every day and realised I hadn't for at least two and this time he wasn't quite the same. We sat down and discussed the bid, he was more formal than usual and asked me a lot of questions. After a short while he became more relaxed and we reverted to our more usual less formal dialogue. I asked him why he'd come and his answer, whatever it was, didn't convince me.

As Dave was leaving I overheard him say to Dave Parkin, "I think Dave's okay." I owe Dave Parkin an explanation and apology. If things hadn't come back when they did, I'd probably have been taken to hospital and filled with prescription drugs.

I'd discussed this event with a number of people and no one had offered me an explanation so I put it down to stress but never believed it was, it was just another of a number of bizarre events in my life.

Then 12 years later in August 2010 it happened again, this time driving north on the M5. I'd been to London and left my car with Ben, our second son, who lived near Kilburn Tube Station. I was running late as the traffic had been horrendous and decided to do the last part of the journey by tube.

I had a new metallic silver, C Class Mercedes 220 Sport, it had wide wheels and flared wheel arches. Ben asked if he could use the car to go the gym and I said he could. On my return, the front offside wheel arch had gouges and a distinct lack of silver paint. I investigated the stone gatepost where I found it.

I didn't make too much of it as Ben was totally distraught, he hadn't taken into account the flare on the wheel arch when he reversed out of his drive.

It was about three hours later that I realised I'd lost time synchronisation again, I didn't know where I was driving to. Was I driving home or going to London? I was driving north so I must be going home but is that right? I should be going to a meeting in London, have I had the meeting or not?

Then I thought if I go to London I mustn't let Ben borrow the car, he'll scratch the wheel arch, but has he already? I really didn't know. Then the episode in Broadway came to mind and I wondered if I was safe to drive. Fortunately there was a sign telling me it was only a few miles to the next services. I'd totally lost any understanding of past, present and future so I focused on driving and wondered if I was safe to be behind the wheel.

I came off the motorway at the Frankley services, parked the car and got out to examine the wheel arch. I was so relived to see the mess it was in. I got back in the car and tried to focus but everything was leaving me. I was becoming more and more confused in exactly the same way I had been 12 years earlier.

Fortunately, inside those 12 years I'd done my first NLP course and taken additional advanced hypnosis training. I was now considerably better prepared and the solution was so simple.

I said quietly to myself, "Okay unconscious mind, there is something we need to address but I don't have time for this now, please can we do this on Saturday afternoon?"

A few seconds later everything started coming back, I'm sat in my car thinking to myself once again, "what on earth is going on".

On Saturday afternoon I prepared myself, telling my unconscious mind I was ready and relaxing into a meditative state. I waited, and waited some more, nothing. After an hour I gave up and it took five years before I had my next episode.

Owen listened to my account of these events and simply said, "You know time is an illusion, that everything happens simultaneously, that time is not linear, so why are you confused? All you did is step outside time."

Suddenly it didn't seem so confusing, Owen's simple response held the key. I then also recalled what Zak had said about how psychics see the most probable outcome as bubbles of possibility in the energy field. I was seeing all the bubbles, possible outcomes without recognising what I was seeing.

I also realise why I didn't recognise what was happening to me, it was fear. At Broadway I was frightened that I was losing my mind. Again on the M5, I didn't accept it and didn't want it.

It happened again in September 2015, it was a morning after I'd taken magic mushrooms. I'd taken the mushrooms at around 7pm and by 10am the following morning the effects had gone. However I was still in a very tranquil and calm state, really appreciating nature. As I'm sat looking at the beauty around me I noticed I was losing time synchronisation again. Then I was asked how the experience was and I realised 'here we go again'. This time I just accepted it. The acceptance brought the realisation that this was truly living in the moment, in the now.

It is difficult to put an explanation as to what happened, as I do not understand it. However I have a hypothesis that it is again to do with energy fields. I feel my consciousness had gone into the etheric field and that the etheric field carries a lot more information than that of the physical body. Indeed this also aligns with what Zak explained about bubbles of possibilities.

Dr Sue Morter explains such a lot but I feel there is so much more information held in the etheric field than we realise. Dr Rupert Sheldrake takes the description of energy fields a lot further and his description could well hold the answer.

Rupert Sheldrake The morphogenetic Universe (1 hour 20 minutes)

In this YouTube video *The Morphogenetic Universe*, Sheldrake explains how birds flock in flight and how fish shoal in the sea. Both these events require simultaneous stimuli, something they are all sensing at exactly the same time.

Sheldrake also describes how the same chemical building blocks create different living structures. It's his contention that it's all to do with fields.

My time disorientation experience also ties in with sacred geometry and what Ayahuasca showed me with vibration and the toroid where everything happens simultaneously. Our 3D heads cannot get themselves around such a thing as time being an illusion; it's a total paradox. Yet when I had my Nirvana experience with Zulf and Mike, I knew timelessness from a different perspective.

Sheldrake's video also provides evidence of human telepathy and telepathy between the owners and their pets. He explains that dogs know when their owners are coming home; it's when the intent to return is set. It's all to do with understanding the energy fields we both create and sense.

When we step outside the convention that we are solid and consider that everything, absolutely everything is only energy vibrating, then we see the universe differently. Many energy fields vibrating at different frequencies, their harmonic resonances create nodes that when linked form geometric shapes that we perceive as solid. Sacred geometry holds the key to the universe. It all becomes so much simpler with no need for complex mathematic formulae. It's all there right in front of us, just look at nature.

I was being shown, I was having the experiences of reality from many different perspectives and with this I was beginning to know that things went a lot deeper than we realise through the limitation of our five senses. The more I was getting to know, the more I understood how little I knew.

13 A Step towards … what?

So Zak had been right, the Ayahuasca was timely and there had been and was continuing internal development. There was just one problem though. While I was very happy on the inside, on the outside everything remained the same and I was concerned that I lacked motivation to 'do' something. So even though I was more convinced than ever that 'just being' held the answer, I was still looking for some 'doing'.

My internal debate about being and doing took on another level because however much one is walking the spiritual path, our 3D world requires money. I began to understand why some people just opted out and became hermits or join a monastery.

I have no interest in material wealth, making money isn't and never has been my driver. When I was in the commercial world I thought it was what I wanted but inside I've never been too interested in money. Money doesn't create happiness although we are conditioned to believe it will. One thing for sure though, lack of money can create stress.

It had been 18 months since I'd seen the psychic Nicola Pierson so I thought it would be timely to see her again. I needed to find my motivation, so I emailed her. The universe, or my guides, had however decided it was time for another intervention. It would be so much easier if they used email.

Further confusion

Inadvertently I'd mailed Christine Pearson in London and set up a meeting with her thinking it was in Nicola's home in Dubai. Such a stupid mistake, a bit like climbing a ladder that's not safe.

Nicola had told me she was moving back to England so when Christine asked if I was now in London I misread the whole thing. I thought Nicola was now in London, whereas she was actually only a few miles away.

So with no Nicola, my plan to speak to a trusted psychic failed.

However Owen recommended an Australian psychic he'd used on occasion and found her to be very reliable and accurate. "She can be very direct though," Owen said. "She doesn't pull her punches."

With the assistance of Skype, I had a reading with Melinda Adams arranged and there was about to be an earthquake in David's life. The ground did move even when the source was over 7,000 miles away.

There is six hours time difference between Dubai and Brisbane so between 7 and 8am on Wednesday 25 June 2014, 'them upstairs' decided that I could do with another nudge. Thankfully, this nudge didn't involve a ladder.

Melinda speaks with an Australian accent. What a surprise but oddly it was. I don't know why but I wasn't expecting to hear an Australian accent.

She began by asking me what was it I was seeking to learn and for any background I considered appropriate. I explained very briefly what had been happening to me and where I was consciously. It didn't take Melinda long to start and once she did it was non-stop, for the best part of 40 minutes she didn't seem to take a breath.

Fortunately I recorded the session as there was so much it would have been impossible to remember it all.

Melinda had tuned in and was telling me pretty directly what I would be doing. She said there were more "shifts in consciousness" to come. Four more shifts to be exact and these would enable me to decide when I wished to step out of my body and walk away, to physically die. Two of these shifts would occur very close together.

She told me about my healing hands and how powerful they were. Not only Reiki, I was also pulling down "inter-dimensional energy". She said, "you are a healer and teacher", which is exactly what Christine had elicited during the soul regression 18 months earlier but Melinda gave a lot of additional detail.

She said, "The first thing you must do is write a book; you have everything you need." She told me I would travel and open a retreat to which many would come long distances, not to spend hours but days, this and a lot more.

I saw all the differing elements of my life and experiences as small individual pieces of a huge jigsaw, it was as if they were all laid out in front of me and at last, for the very first time in my entire life, I was shown the lid of the box and what a picture it was. When I saw it, and understood it, there was a dawning recognition, I'd always known but didn't realise I did.

I felt the inner desire, that deep motivation I'd lacked for so long. Everything Melinda said resonated, it vibrated through me as if I was huge bell being give one hell of a whack.

This was just two months since taking Ayahuasca and meeting Siobhan at Stonehenge yet within these two months there had been more realisations and now it was time to do something with it all. I had a plan, an objective and I'd be doing what I enjoy and find easy. At last I had motivation for 'doing'.

There was a lot to take in from what Melinda said so I decided to let things settle and not run off in any one of several possible directions. I thought I'd just ponder on things just for a few days. As I did, more detail behind what Melinda had said emerged in my mind and the enormity of it all became just a little overwhelming, it was good ego food and I wondered if ego was then playing its hand.

I started questioning what I'd been told and questioning myself. The dreaded inner dialogue set off once more, questioning and challenging. It's like having a follower who just questions, sets doubt and sometimes will not shut up. The logical head was in opposition to the intuitive feeling self. In meditation I felt Melinda was spot on, exactly right but logically how could she be?

I decided to have another word with Zak, looking for confirmation but the session didn't bring me what I expected. He did however confirm that Melinda was certainly no charlatan. He told me again that from here on in there would be more lustre in my life; that everything would work out. He said again I must consider this not a new chapter but a new book and that I wasn't to close the door on any possibility, just to focus on one.

It half helped but half didn't. There had been nothing specific but then again Zak usually isn't. His 'new book' I still considered as a metaphor and didn't consider his reference to be an actual book. It never crossed my mind.

It was a few days later that Sue told me that she'd seen Nicola's husband in the supermarket and that Nicola was in Dubai. I checked my email to discover my mistake. The thing is, I don't believe it was a mistake. Just like the ladder, I was just following guidance. It was guidance that took me to Melinda, the universe had decided. Nicola being in Dubai did though represent an opportunity for a confirmation of what Melinda had said so I contacted Nicola and arranged a visit.

I explained I'd had a reading from Melinda and that I was looking for confirmation and hence wouldn't explain what I had been told. The challenge was set and accepted. Nicola used Tarot and the confirmation could not be more explicit, startling, and for those that know Tarot a lot of major arcana cards and all very positive.

Afterwards I told Nicola what Melinda had said and she said there had not been one negative card, nothing saying "stop, wake up and smell the coffee", nothing at all. "Go for it David, it's there for you, all of it" she said.

I knew I had to write a book and what it would be about and then realised Zak had said this wasn't a new chapter, it was a new book. It finally dawned on me.

I'd started writing four years earlier and submitted the first three chapters to a publisher for it to be politely rejected. I looked once more at what I'd written and it didn't take long to realise I needed to start all over again, this was really going to be a totally new book.

This led me to consider once again what else Zak had said. He was telling me about the book, the first thing Melinda had said I should do, Melinda said a lot more and Zak was telling me not to limit myself by focusing only on one thing, there was a lot of other equally rewarding possibilities.

Things were again about to change, and again significantly, there were more possibilities

Sitting as we did regularly at JamaicaBlue café, Owen and I were chatting away merrily about I recall not what. It was one of many conversations we had about many topics, however on this occasion and seemingly out of the blue, Owen said, "I see you in Peru." This came as a surprise as I'd never considered Peru. I knew nothing about it and had little interest in learning, so I ignored his statement and moved on.

However Owen followed up and said he knew someone in Peru, Tracie, he explained she runs an Ayahuasca retreat and he'd put us in contact. I said something like thanks but never for one moment thought anything would come of it. I'd done an Ayahuasca and if I wanted to do it again I didn't need to go to South America.

A few days later I'm going to Carol's and as she opened the door she said to me, "As I was opening the door I saw you moving to Peru?" I said, "Have you been talking to Owen?" "No, why?" She replied.

A few more days pass, this time I'm in Dubai Marina Mall with a friend Yazan, who's a shaman, we're chatting away and suddenly he says, "Did you know your destiny is Peru?"
"Oh my god," I said. "Have you been speaking to Owen?"
"No, why?" he replied.
"Carol?" I enquired.
"No," he said.

I was not slow picking this up. These three conversations were in less than two weeks so I thought I had better take this seriously. However the cost of flights to Peru was just a little restrictive so I didn't take any action.

Then I received an email from the estate agent who was selling my mother's house. They asked if I could get the house cleared by 1 November, which was just a few weeks away. Steph had offered to clear it for me but it'd been my family home for nearly 60 years and I felt it was something I should do, but Steph's offer was very enticing. A day later another email, this time from the solicitors. Would I be returning to sign the house sale papers or should they be couriered?

I'd always bought my air tickets London – Dubai – London so I could return home, sort out the house, sign the papers and then go to Peru. A couple of weeks had passed and no email from Peru though. I hadn't made any decision and time was passing, if I was to go back I had to make a decision quickly.

Then as if miraculously an email from Peru, Tracie had a retreat from the 10th to the 20th of November. It seemed the decision had been made for me. Within a few days I was back in the UK and then what seemed so quickly on my way to Peru.

A month or so earlier, Peru had not been in my conscious awareness. Now I'm off half way around the world because three people had said 'Peru'. All I knew about Peru could be written on less than one side of A4 paper.

14 Iquitos, Peru

Iquitos is in the Amazon jungle, close to the boarder with Brazil, it is the largest town in the world that is not accessible by road. There are a few cars and plenty of Motorkars, that are converted motorbikes with two rear wheels. A single Motokar is loud but en masse they are a cacophony.

Iquitos is probably the greatest possible contrast to Dubai. The two cities are 9,000 miles apart but are polar opposites. The retreat is an hour by Motokar into the jungle, where there is no electricity, no mobile phone network coverage and no internet. It has plenty of insects though. This was a change of surroundings.

I'd booked my flights to arrive in Iquitos just six days before the start of the retreat. My intention was to spend sometime on the Amazon and get a feel for the surroundings.

I arrived on the 4th of November 2014 and stayed at La Casona, a hotel that Tracie recommended. Not five star, nothing in Iquitos is but it was clean and the staff friendly.

The first night I was there I discovered Tracie was staying in the same hotel and the following morning we met for breakfast. We chatted easily and she suggested that there was little for me in Iquitos so why didn't I come out to jungle straight away? The following day I did.

The Amazon Jungle

I arrived at the Phoenix Ayahuasca on Thursday 6th of November 2014 four days before the retreat officially started.

My first night in the jungle was louder than I had anticipated. Having no electricity is not a problem, torches and candles suffice admirably, however when I blew out the candle beside my bed, the dark was truly dark.

The heavy clouds and rain blocked out any moonlight whatsoever, the wildlife seemed to be partying, it was very loud and a new experience. I listened for a while then dropped off to sleep.

The jungle seems to bring its own peace and tranquillity. I was the only guest, Tracie and her brother Mark made me very welcome and I felt really chilled. It is different to being in Iquitos, although a small town it still had its attractions and things 'to do'.

Sitting on their veranda looking at trees is all there was to do, this was the capital of chill, calm reflection with ample opportunity just to be. I found myself slipping into a meditative state without intent or even recognition. Oh if everybody could experience this, no pressure, no stress, time and the structures we create by wearing a watch could not interfere, no one else to consider, no plans, nothing. The next significant event would be nightfall.

It was four days before the formal start of the retreat. Never before in my life have I had so much time with nothing, absolutely nothing 'to do'. No coffee shops, no internet, nowhere to go visit. I felt everything slow down and yet time didn't drag, exactly the opposite, it just flew by.

Before I'd settled into this environment, very early on, I decided to finish a book I was reading on my iPad. I was sat on the veranda when I noticed a young boy appear from the jungle, at a guess I'd say he was seven or eight years old. He seemed to take an interest in me, sitting there alone. He had with him an old tennis ball. He came to stand near and just look at me. I smiled at him and moved over slightly so he could sit next to me, which he did.

I showed him my iPad and launched a simple App a little like Tetris. I did a few moves and handed him the iPad. He didn't take it. He just looked at me as if I was mad, showed me his bald ball and left. Then the children of the London Slum in Nakuru came to mind and I realised I'd fallen into the trap of the Western mind. I gave myself a talking to.

A few days later the other guests arrived, there were eight of us. Eight people about to embark on the most profound personal development experience of their lives. It is not for everyone, it takes courage to embark on such a journey.

Interestingly there were six Americans. It seems that Ayahuasca is better known and understood in the US than in Europe.

Tobacco

The first event was a tobacco purge and fortunately I had no idea what I was setting myself up for. If I'd known I doubt I'd have participated.

Tobacco is considered a master teacher plant. It is drunk, not smoked. The tobacco is boiled and distilled into a liquor and foul tasting it was. Tobacco consumed in this manner absorbs toxins or 'bad energies', it removes things that are not serving us by creating a purge, which is vomiting that occurs after about 10 to 15 minutes.

I'd done so much personal development, or so I'd arrogantly thought so I set my intention to really shift some stuff with this session so I asked the plant to go deep. It was no good playing round the edges, I thought, lets do this properly! Oh David, why?

Within an hour most people had finished. I was vomiting for at least eight hours. It was one of the most unpleasant experiences of my life. I felt absolutely awful and had by far the worst experience of everyone. Later, when everyone else was eating dinner, I was in bed. My last purge was at 11pm.

The following day I felt retched. I ate breakfast and started to feel better but the taste of tobacco lingered. It took another day to get rid of it. From everything I did, tobacco was by far the most difficult. I should not have set my intention like I did, I'll never do it again.

Wachuma

The following day we did Wachuma. It is a plant medicine made from a cactus and happily there was no vomiting but I felt I didn't really get the most out of the experience due to the lingering tobacco.

For more than 4,000 years Wachuma has been used in Peru for the purposes of healing, divination, and expanding consciousness. It's said to be a doorway to the spirit world, which is why it's named after Saint Peter who, according to Christian mythology, holds the keys to the gates of heaven.

A Wachuma ceremony is said to bring about a shift in our consciousness. It helps us to heal from the past and open to a more heart centred way of living.

The others in my group reported feeling at one with nature and 'seeing' things through a different set of eyes. Sadly, due to the tobacco I missed it. Little did I know then how this cacti works and how much it would later impact my life.

Sapo or Kambo frog medicine

Our next ceremony was with Sapo, which is a little green venomous frog only found in the Amazon. The venom is secreted and harvested with no harm to the frog. It has been used for centuries by the indigenous tribes of the Amazon, amongst a variety of other things it enhances the senses, all become more sensitive, this is very useful for hunters.

The Sapo treatment took five days, three treatments with a day between each. Before each treatment we drank two litres of water.

An incense stick was used to create three burns on my upper arm. These burns blister quickly and the blister is picked off leaving a small hole with open blood vessels. These holes were filled with the Sapo venom. It doesn't sound fun and it's not!

Within a few minutes, I began to feel light headed and headed off to the toilet. My temperature went sky high and I felt my face was burning off. I was sweating what seemed to be slime; it wasn't normal sweat it seemed thicker and there was such a lot of it. I soon became very nauseous and vomited several times. I was dizzy holding on to the side of the toilet with one hand and my vomit bowl with the other. The vomiting was supplemented with diarrhoea and I thought to myself what on earth am I doing this for?

Very soon though, my head cleared and my temperature came down. The sweating, vomiting and diarrhoea all stopped as suddenly as they had started. A cold shower was a delight. The whole thing lasted less than 15 minutes and awful as it sounds and was, it was worth it. Within half an hour I felt vibrant, really alive and so full of energy. Everyone else said they felt the same.

The second session was two days later. This was five burns and this time the symptoms were proportionally stronger and I thought I was going to die but afterwards again there was recognition it was worth it.

The third and last session was seven burns and this time I didn't think I would die, I knew it. I think I partially lost consciousness but obviously I didn't die. Afterwards such a feeling for life such an appreciation, feeling so physically well, literally I felt on top of the world.

So why do people, and lots of them, do this? Sapo enhances the immune system; giving it a real boost. It is a powerful medicine against snakebites, yellow fever, malaria and other epidemic diseases. Scientific research into Sapo started in the 1980s. Nominated for a Nobel Prize for his research into Sapo, Italian scientist Vittorio Erspamer of the University of Rome wrote that "the secretion contains a fantastic chemical cocktail with potential medical applications, unequalled by any other amphibian".

A more thorough scientific explanation of this wonderful frog medicine can be found in the appendices.

Ayahuasca

In the evening of the third day we prepared for the first Ayahuasca ceremony. A native shaman called Cecelia came. She doesn't speak English but Tracie and Mark translated. In all there were four Ayahuasca sessions planned and I did three.

We all went to the Maloka, a purpose built round building about 8 metres across. There was a type of alter where Mark who presided sat. One by one we went to Mark who handed us the foul tasting medicine.

In the first ceremony, Mother Ayahuasca told me quite emphatically "you will not find the answers you are seeking here". I had no idea if 'here' was Iquitos or Ayahuasca. It did though still show me a lot.

First, there was a very detailed orgy. Lots of people engaged in sex in lots of different ways. It wasn't at all erotic, just lots of people doing sex. When I acknowledged how pointless it all seemed I moved on.

Next, there was a portal seemingly into the universe that just took me in circles. I went through it and the other side was from where I'd started, I did it time and time again always returning to the same place.

Then there was a head with a laughing face wearing what must have been a hundred hats. These hats were being removed very quickly using left then right then left hands repeatedly; as each hat was removed a new one emerged. When the hat changed so did the face and all the time laughing. I recognised each face was a different facet of me. Everything was me, no matter what face emerged it was always me.

This was nothing like my first Ayahuasca experience. All this seemed to be about me and it went on for a while and I found it just a little boring.

The second ceremony was more enlightening. Again there were lots of colourful images morphing continually into different things. The one that stood out the most being a staircase that was continually changing into different, more elaborate and grand staircases going very high.

Towards the end of this second ceremony I sensed a number of people around me, one to my left and four at my feet. It was very dark but I opened my eyes and there was just sufficient light to realise no one was there, so I closed them again and sensed the four at my feet had their backs to me and were moving away and the one to my left had gone.

I called the beings at my feet back asking them if they were my guides. They laughed and then morphed into four fingers of a left hand around the neck of a guitar. Then one said, "we're fingers playing your tune".

My interpretation of this is that I create the notes, the vibration and they play them to the universe. So I create the vibration via my guides. This is not how I'd previously interpreted the guide's work but the more I reflected on it, the more sense it made.

Our unconscious mind creates our reality, the guide's work to our tune to set the vibration in the universe to manifest what our unconscious creates. Well, that's my present interpretation. On the surface, it may seem to contradict other interpretations I have for how the guides work, but that is what I was shown and how I've interpreted it.

The third ceremony was again lots of beautiful images but this is not what I wanted so I kept going through them and behind all there was me. No matter where I went it was me. I asked for the images to be taken away and they were, until I let them back again. All I found behind everything was me.

I put all the images behind me and set my focus on self rather than them. I saw myself lying out as if through my eyes other than they were closed, my right arm became fidgety. As I lay there with my eyes closed I saw the etheric energy field of my right arm rise out of the body and I immediately panicked and it returned. I relaxed and it happened again. I saw the opportunity for my awareness and my full etheric field to follow it and fear rushed through me, I didn't want this to happen.

I felt that if I'd let my full etheric field and my awareness leave my body, I'd leave David Walton behind. All the things I held dear would be gone. All the individual experiences that formed the ego of self would be lost. I was full of fear and didn't have the courage to go on that journey.

I declined the fourth ceremony, I'd reflected on what Mother Ayahuasca had said and I didn't want these morphing images anymore. I did though go to the ceremony and meditated whilst the others drank the medicine. This was a very powerful meditation. I had lots of colours that I'd not had in mediation before, not images; just mosaics of colour that I realised were a distraction.

Once I started on the concept of distraction I realised everything is a distraction. All the things we find on this physical manifest plain is nothing but pure distraction and is keeping us away from the reality of truly being. The more I realised this the deeper and more profound it became until I recognised the ultimate truth, I am my own distraction.

Ego distracts, my ego is my own limiting factor in my spiritual progression.

I certainly had a lot to consider. What was Ayahuasca saying to me, where would I find my answers?

Disappearance of the Universe

We learn in many different ways, from our parents, our formal education our friends, through reading etc. it never stops. On retreats it is the same, we learn from the formal planned part and the experience of the plants. We learn from those around us, the other participants and from books that may have been recommended.

Tracie and I spent a lot of time talking about spirituality; I found the conversations fascinating especially when she explained how she'd overcome alcoholism and a heroin addiction. Like myself Tracie had had her own deeply profound spiritual experiences before she met the plants. Tracie was very interested in learning about my experiences and recommended that I read *Disappearance of the Universe* by Gary R Renard. She hit the mark it is one of those books I just could not put down. It is one of the best books I have ever read. I've now read it twice, and need to read it again.

Disappearance leads to *A Course in Miracles* written and edited by Helen Schucman and William Thetford. It is a self-study curriculum to bring about what it calls a "spiritual transformation" and Schucman claims that an "inner voice", which she identified as Jesus, guided her writing.

In *Disappearance,* two people, Arten and Pursah materialise in Gary's living room. They were once Thomas and Thaddeus two of Jesus's disciples. They come many times and the book is about what they taught Gary. Arten and Pursah explain that todays Christianity is not what Jesus taught and if he were preaching today he'd be considered a heretic. They also explain the reason for creation and free will. They said God did not create the universe, it was created by Christ in a divine accident, wondering about the concept of separation from God.

One of the explanations in the book I resonate with is oneness. The soul is unity, it see's though our eyes and every other person's eyes simultaneously. Every time we judge, make critical comment then soul see's this as criticism of self, the unconscious ego see's it as what we believe of ourselves and consequently provides it.

The universe provides for us what we asked for, every simple unkind or judging thought, returns to us a more thorough explanation of karma.

Karma

Karma is not retribution or a punishment. Karma provides learning. If you do something that impacts others, then how do you know what that impact is? You know by understanding that feeling, by being the receiver. This is true learning.

Just imagine what would happen if one morning all the employees of the world's financial markets woke up with a profound knowing of 'what goes around comes around' and 'sow as you shall reap'.

Suddenly they realise that manipulating the markets for their own benefit to the detriment of millions of people carries karma multiplied by the same millions. If this life is not a one-off hit, then the time will come for them to understand the implications of their actions by feeling the impact it had on others.

The higher our vibration the more aware we become, the more caring we become, the more forgiving we become and hence we can see karma for what it is and it no longer impacts our lives.

What I'm advocating, through my experiences that are Buddhist in nature, is not what those who control our society and that wish to maintain the status quo wish to hear.

When we recognise that we come back time and time again, that life isn't random, then the question of why automatically arises. For what purpose do we return to experience life on Earth over and over again?

Every single one of us has a purpose. We planned it ourselves. Life is not random; we are not victims of circumstance. This is what I know as this is what I've been shown and experienced and what I set out to explain by the end of this book.

Disappearance had a real impact, it is a deeply profound book and one I highly recommend.

I left Iquitos so thankful that I had gone. Tracie taught me a lot although I was somewhat confused by Mother Ayahuasca, just where would I find my answers? My next stop was Cusco, home of the Inca Empire.

Cusco

I didn't know a single person in Cusco although Tracie had provided an introduction to Rory, who runs a retreat at the other side of Cusco to where I was staying. I had fortunately picked a hotel very close to Plaza de Armes, which is a historical centre and central tourist attraction. I was immediately enchanted.

I spent a few days doing the normal touristy things including the obligatory visit to Machu Picchu. Such a beautiful place but to me it lacked the feeling element and for all the hype I was just a little disappointed. On the other hand, the citadel of Sacsayhuaman, located just to the north of Cusco, held an energy I could feel. For energy sensitive people I'd recommend it over Machu Picchu. That said, you can hardly go to Cusco without going to Machu Picchu, it's obligatory and remarkably beautiful.

There are a lot of very interesting places in Cusco although I don't agree with some of the standard explanations found in tourist guidebooks. Like the explanation of staggering skill of the

Incan masons who somehow built huge walls from stones that have been cut and shaped so precisely like a big stone jigsaw puzzle. The most famous example is the 12-angled stone that has drawn thousands of visitors.

I was staying only 100 yards away from the impressive 12-angled stone.

According to traditional science, I am expected to accept that this stone was cut using nothing more than bronze chisels and stone hammers. The smoothness and accuracy of the sides formed by rubbing with finely crushed stone to create a type of sandpaper.

Considering the size, considerable weight and logistics of transport, the number of people involved and the countless thousands upon thousands of similar, if not as complex, stones I just do not accept it. It had to be easier than what we are told. Who's in a box here, is it me or is it the archaeologists?

I'd been in Cusco around a week and as soon as Rory's retreat was over he called and invited me around. Rory is what I would call a typical Yorkshire man. We chatted to find we had a lot in common and Rory suggested we did Wachuma together.

I thought it'd be a good idea as my previous experience in Iquitos had not been good. The following day I arrived at 8am and by 9am we started. There was someone else there as well, an American woman called Maria. I had no idea how our relationship would progress.

Wachuma strikes

What I didn't expect is the miserable journey I had. Lots of purging, shaking and generally feeling totally retched. Once you start on a medicine journey you cannot cut it short. I swore I'd never do Wachuma again and Rory found that most amusing.

A couple of days later I had a sense of wellbeing, an inner sense of comfort and it came to me that the miserable experience had actually done something. Rory told me the plant was working on things on the inside, deep-seated stuff. I still rather arrogantly thought that all my inside stuff had already been done, how wrong I was.

Back in my daily life I quickly settled into my old routine of coffee shops. There are a number overlooking the beautiful Plaza de Armes and one in particular I really enjoyed; their coffee was reasonable as was their WiFi. I'd read the papers and done the standard email and Facebook stuff. Then just looked at the Plaza and people watched. One day after the standard routine, I felt especially calm and when I settle, really settle, things can happen, and happen they did.

A softly spoken voice said to me, "you've come home". I felt both calm and surprised as then it said, "this is where you live". I turned round to look if there was someone behind me and there wasn't. I just sat and realised that inside I felt that what I'd just heard seemed to resonate with me at a deep level and I felt it was truth.

I then realised that I was already planning the logistics of an early return to Dubai. It just seemed that the decision had been made, all in less than a minute.

Following one's intuition can shake things up and my thinking head had it's say, mainly about the costs involved in leaving Dubai and selling my car that was less than five months old, selling all my furniture, etc.

However despite this left brain chatter, I cut short my trip and leaving a suitcase with Rory and returned to Dubai. As I dropped the suitcase off, Rory said to me, "go straight to Dubai, do not stop in England". He was quite firm but I took no notice.

My air ticket was back to London and I had then to buy a return to Dubai. As it transpired, the first weekend after I landed, Steph was planning a pre-Christmas party as Ben, our middle one, was going to Australia with his partner Kimberley for Christmas.

"What a wonderful coincidence," I thought. Only to be devastated to find out I wasn't invited. This caused some difficult words between Steph and I and I even contemplated going north anyway and staying in a local hotel. These unsavoury thoughts that just emerge, the thinking mind at its worst. I quickly sent them on their way.

I finally asked Steph why she was being so cruel and she explained that she didn't want "my energy" as it would cause her stress. She'd planned this party between her family and the children and for her, having me there would not work. I understood this as soon as she said "energy", however I wish I'd gone straight to Dubai as Rory had suggested and saved myself the distress.

It was sometime later that a thought came to mind about what
Steph had said about "my energy". What came to mind was the
distress Steph had gone through the weekend of the Queens
Golden Jubilee and she was avoiding putting herself in a similar
position. Whether this is right or wrong I do not know but it is a
mental construct that makes it easier for me to deal with.

However following my acceptance that I was not going north I
made plans to return to Dubai. It was 3pm on Thursday 4
December 2014 when I sent a mail to friends saying I'd be back
at 8am the following morning. To one in particular this must
have caused apoplexy. I caught the 8pm flight from London and
arrived at 7.30am on Friday the 5th of December.

I got a taxi to my apartment to find that in my absence it had
been sub-let. The moment I walked in I was greeted by the
extremely strong smell of cigarettes. My whole apartment
literally reeked of cigarettes, not nice for someone who doesn't
smoke.

As I looked round, there was a set of additional bedding on one
sofa. Clearly there had been two people living there, not one. In
the fridge there were things I would never buy, a particular
brand of butter and the carton was nearly empty, which I took to
mean that this stay hadn't just been a day or two. There were
three toilet roll cardboard inners in the guest bathroom and two
in the en-suite confirmed that. In the kitchen waste bin was an
empty packet of Virginia Gold tobacco. My candle holders had
been used as ashtrays and been poorly cleaned, there was more
but that summarises it.

Of all the things, it was the smell that I found the most difficult to
deal with, it was so strong and the realisation that whoever had
been there had only just left. We could have missed each other
by moments. When I texted the key holder, it took over six hours
to get a response and all I got was denial after denial, the barrage
of lies were so easy to see through. An apology would have been
enough to move on, but the denials capped things off for me.

The apartment was special. It had been the first place I'd ever furnished myself, the first place I'd called my own, ever. It was here that I'd made so many inner discoveries, a place I really enjoyed. If there had been the remotest chance of changing my mind about leaving Dubai, it was now truly smashed. The universe was making doubly sure, belt and braces.

I sold my car and furniture and left Dubai on 31 January 2015, exactly one calendar year since my fall. I was leaving behind the life I'd rebuilt after our separation. I didn't know what I was going to find but in my heart, it felt right.

When I left England three years earlier, I was running away. Now I felt very strongly that I was running toward… something.

As if to give me some additional confirmation, Virgin Atlantic upgraded me to Business Class. Everything happens for a reason I thought. I was about to start an adventure into the unknown and what an adventure it would be.

Part 3

Peru

More change

15 Cusco again

I arrived back in Cusco on the15th of February 2015 and booked into the same hotel I was in 10 weeks earlier. It was easy enough to pick up where I left off but somehow things felt different. The first few days had me slip down the vibrational ladder as my thinking head asked some very pertinent questions. "What on earth are you doing here, you don't speak the language, you know one person and he's on the other side of Cusco, you have no plans. Why have you come?"

All reasonable and very valid questions. The light, happy mood I'd become so accustomed to had slipped. Fortunately I had Skype and a half reasonable WiFi connection so I spoke to Owen and got some sage advice that helped put things in perspective. "David, you've not been there a week yet, give it time. Get yourself an apartment and settle, meditate", he said. It was sound advice but it didn't change my then state of mind. However within three weeks I'd found an apartment and things began to look up.

I'd just moved in to my new place when Rory called, he was planning another Wachuma session and would I like to come. I said 'yes' immediately and then I remembered the previous experiences and I questioned myself about the wisdom of repeating Wachuma, I went anyway.

Rory mixed the cactus powder with grapefruit and lime, about a 12 ounce glass, not the sort of thing you'd order but not really unpleasant. We drank and waited.

And waited I did. It was exactly 8am when I took the medicine and at 10.30am I was wondering if I should get a book out. Others seemed in a deep peaceful space but I felt exactly the same as I had at 8am. So I waited some more. There was really nothing else I could do. I had no nausea just a degree of boredom.

At about 11am I started to feel cold, there was a lot of cloud cover and no sun, I only had a t-shirt and light summer jacket so I went to the room that had been offered to me if I needed to lie down. The room seemed colder than outside so I got under the duvet and waited, I didn't have to wait long.

I got colder and colder and then began to shiver. It was as if my bones were cold and it reminded me of my first Ayahuasca experience nearly a year earlier.

I was so cold I was shaking and I recalled what I'd been told the previous year, to 'let go', but of what? This must have been going on for over half an hour and I wasn't getting any warmer. I just abandoned myself to the cold and then the recognition of what letting go was. I recalled a line from *Disappearance of the Universe*, about "being one" and everything else is an illusion that we create. It just went around and around in my head.

The moment I accepted it was an illusion and turned my thinking head off so I could just 'be', in an instant the cold vanished. I wasn't now warm though, I just didn't have a temperature to gauge; there was no 'hot or cold'. As soon as I recognised that and thought about it, I was back freezing again. So I visualised myself as the light and as if turned off by a switch the cold instantaneously vanished. However, as soon as I recognised the cold had gone, wham, it was back. I was in and out of this a few times before I stopped the thinking, recognition process and remained in the state of comfort of 'being'. In this space is the peace and tranquillity I so enjoy. I wasn't on a bed in a retreat in Peru, I just was.

Then an inner voice said to me, "you will not find the warmth you seek from the material world, those covers hide truth".

This had once more engaged the thinking process, however I did not return to the freezing state, just an awareness of temperature and I was just slightly cool.

It was noon and I heard people downstairs so I got up. I was uncertain on my feet and took one step at a time, I felt totally spaced out and welcomed the tea I was offered. I didn't have much to say, in fact I didn't really feel like speaking, I seemed in a half way house between the peace and tranquillity of where I'd just been and the physical.

There were three of us sat on the grass, all calm and tranquil. We were talking about states of being however I was somewhat confused, I understood the state I had experienced but was unable to find the words to express it. I just stopped and went into a semi trance. After a few moments, the trance developed into an emotional state and I recalled Steph and the tears began to flow.

This was a real surprise I really couldn't understand it. I'd thought I was over everything to do with the marriage. I had no desire for reconciliation and was happy with the relationship that had developed, both of us moving on. Then suddenly there were tears rolling down my face and I had no idea why other than I knew it was about Steph.

Seemingly in unison Rory and Maria both said "let go" and I thought, "what am I hanging on to?" I let the thought hang without looking for an answer. Then a new realisation arose and an uncomfortable one it was.

What came back was the Ayahuasca experience in Iquitos where I recognised my etheric body moving out of my physical body and the fear that created. The fear created by ego was, as I thought, the pending loss of David Walton, the loss of ego and what ego hangs onto. Moving on means letting go of everything that we hold dear and this is also our children, and they encompassed part of Steph, she represents them to me. Denying my wife is denying my children as in one sense we co-created them.

This was all too much for my mind to analyse. In fact I didn't believe I wanted to analyse it so I went back upstairs for a lie down and to clear my head. For the next hour or so I just relaxed in a deep meditative state, it was beautiful. Then slowly I returned to the physical thinking world.

It was at about 6pm that Rory brought a huge pizza and eating was the final step in the grounding process. I don't think I've ever enjoyed a pizza more.

As Buddha said, "enlightenment comes from letting go of all attachments, as attachments cause suffering". When we drop all judgement and love everyone equally, lifting every living person to the same level as those we hold most dear, then we have let go of ego and then we will find life becomes easier. It sounds easy but as I realised that day letting go is not as easy, I had strings.

Dark night of the soul

A few days later Rory invited me to my first experience with Magic Mushrooms and I was eager to try what are locally called, 'shrooms.

Two types of 'shroom were available, Californian and Hawaiian, the latter being the stronger. I opted for the Californian then I had to decide on the quantity. The standard dose is 3.5 grams however as I know how sensitive I am to Ayahuasca, I decided on 2.5 grams.

I watched as these dried and odd looking fungi were weighed and finely chopped then put in a coffee mug. Next, about two to three ounces of chocolate was also finely chopped and added. Finally, the mug was filled with hot water and I was handed a spoon. I stirred and stirred some more. Left it awhile to cool, stirred again and at 7pm I drank what tasted like hot chocolate, no surprise there then. The only difference was this was a little bitty, I made sure I consumed every last bit.

Rory had a few house rules and number one was no talking, isolation for three hours. I went to lie down in a darkened room.

It took about half an hour before I went cold but this time only slightly, a little later the visions started, they were like Ayahuasca. There was darkness, curling images, serpents with long octopus like tentacles, revolving and evolving into massive spiders with huge fat tentacle ridden legs. I was being taken down deeper into the darkness where more and more of these ever-changing creatures waited.

I wasn't scarred just unsettled. I'd seen similar things when with Erik and knew they would pass. That said, I'd have preferred something more welcoming. I just observed, coloured outlines formed the images, the colours changed as did the degree of brightness and this made them three dimensional and very real, albeit knowingly hallucinatory. There was no way to turn them off my eyes were already shut. Now my body started to move, only slightly but it was moving on it's own.

I watched and after what seemed quite a while, I decided to make them go away. So I told them to go and they did. Then I noticed some new object like images appear to my right so I went towards them and as I got closer they morphed into the original serpents. We played this game several times. I looked at them directly and said, "you don't frighten me, go away". It made no difference. It was dark and uncomfortable, my body movements were due to how uncomfortable I felt, now I wanted it to stop but it wouldn't.

I tried all sorts of things, the going within as I'd done with Wachuma, no impact, not even the feeling of comfort. I was becoming increasing unsettled and told them to "fuck off". They left just long enough for me to think they had, then they returned rapidly. I was so heartily sick of them and I wondered for how long they'd be hanging around. This went on and on for what seemed like ages and I was becoming more and more uncomfortable, my arms and legs were fidgety, my hips moving, I could stop them easily enough but then they'd start again. Now I was becoming very uncomfortable, this was a dark place and it began to absorb me, it just wouldn't stop.

I'm sure this had been going on for well over an hour probably nearer two and I wondered how far away 10pm was, so I opened my eyes, turned on a bedside lamp and looked at my watch, it was 7.45pm. I couldn't believe it, I didn't want to believe it, I felt low, I could hardly face another two hours, which at this rate would seem like a week. To say I was now very uncomfortable was an understatement. My body was writhing, the images would not go away and it felt like it would go on forever, what was I to do?

I just resigned myself to an uncomfortable time then recalled a passage from *Disappearance*, which states that everything, absolutely everything comes from within; it's all a self-created illusion. So as I watched the images swirl around in front of me, I looked at them as if they were part of me. Rather than mentally push them away and reject them, I invited them in with love, understanding and forgiveness. As I did, the swirling slowed down and they began to shrink. They lost their stark contours and their colour; they just melted into my heart. I should have remembered Gill Edward's recommendation with my boulder and what that showed me.

I realised these images, the whole experience, was a metaphor for my deep, very deep down, unconscious fears, fears of which I was totally unaware. In my past, with a combination of ignoring, distraction and willpower coupled with the passage of time, all I had done was to suppress them. That suppression may have happened many years ago and have been well forgotten but to the unconscious they were still as real as they ever were. The 'shrooms had brought them very much into my awareness and I had to find the only way of really dealing with them. I transformed them with the only real tool we have, love.

As I recognised this, other things came to mind, my judgement over the wars in the Middle East. I knew all I could do was to just offer love and forgiveness, to both sides, no judgement and as I did George Bush appeared as real as ever and the whole of the first Iraq war was there. Again, I just offered love and forgiveness and in a flash he went. Next to arrive was Tony Blair and again I knew, deep inside how judgemental I've been so I just offered him love and forgiveness and he went.

Then images of people came who I'd judged and who I'd thought had wronged me. Now I knew deep inside this was not the case as they were hurt long ago and all I am is a reflection of their pain within myself. I'd judged their behaviour without the realisation that it was all to do with me. When we point fingers there are always three pointing right back.

This new knowing didn't even need love and forgiveness as the judgement evaporated so did they, as one went another arrived. This went on a few times then the images stopped, there was stillness. My body was still, my mind was still, there were no images and I felt a deep comfort and with it I sensed a new level of awareness.

I realised how love and forgiveness heals at such a deep and profound level. I knew it was the whole planet than needed love and forgiveness and so I offered it and then just relaxed and entered the beautiful state of 'being'.

It was a while later I heard people in the kitchen. It was 10pm but I had no desire to move, I just lay, settled with a deep comfort and a new awareness. At about 11pm I got up. The kitchen was empty and I helped myself to a large piece of chocolate cake, Rory's second rule is, after 'shrooms, cake!

Hearing people talking outside I went to join them. Although I had no desire to speak although I felt I needed to be with others. I was asked, "how was it?" My only words were "dark and profound."

I certainly felt 'shrooms were magic, it was like many lifetimes of learning in just a few hours. I had no regrets about the initial darkness, it was needed to find the answers I did.

A week later I got another invite from Rory, his retreat was coming to an end and one person had asked for another 'shrooms session before he left, would I like to join? I had not the slightest hesitation. "Yes!" I said. The next round could not have been more different to the first.

"Understanding" a term that doesn't quite cut it

If I had the eloquence of Shakespeare coupled with the vocabulary of Churchill, I still would not be able to accurately describe the experience.

The images started. Huge gigantic towers, every colour imaginable and more, continually morphing into different shapes and evolving in detail like Fibonacci spirals, some going down, some arising, all beautiful and hypnotic. In every direction, these colossal images formed a seemingly infinite number of patterns, objects, buildings, tunnels and branches, all with what seemed an infinite degree of detail.

Wherever I looked there seemed infinite detail. No matter where I focused my attention, it went on and on, like the biggest mosaic one could conceive with each piece being a beautiful image of fantastic detail. If I could have frozen this multi-dimensional experience, taken a snap shot, then never, in years of examination would any particular part of the image be repeated. Everything was new and continually changing, morphing and evolving. This was creation on a scale the human mind cannot comprehend.

When in it, being part of it was beyond awesome. Take the most beautiful image you ever seen, multiple it many times and it would not register on a scale compared with this. It was not of this world, nor the capacity of my imagination to perceive, or now my capability to describe.

I have no idea how long it went on for. I was in no mind to make it stop, I was totally absorbed, fascinated and in awe. Then I wondered, is this a distraction once more, am I missing the point I learnt in Iquitos? So I tried to make it stop. It didn't, not for a moment. So I invited it, all of it inside, to make it part of me, again it hadn't the slightest effect, there was no change at all.

Then I thought, 'was this then outside of me?' and immediately a knowing came that it was not. Although I could not contain it so this posed a conundrum, how could it be separate from and still part of me?

Then the images began to change, the scale seemed to reduce, from infinite to local and around the image there was now darkness. So I went to the darkness and as I did it lit up and there was more to be observed. It was not darkness, it was more areas without light and I realised that where I placed my awareness, where I decided to go, brightness arose, identifying the same awesome images I had previously seen.

I looked for more darkness to explore but no matter where I went everything lit up. It was as if I had a huge mega watt search lamp on my forehead. Then an insight, I was controlling what I was seeing. As I thought of a tunnel down this amazingly intricate tunnel I went, to come out to scenes of expanse but no detail until I turned my attention to an area and it lit up with whatever I thought of.

This left me confused as earlier everything was happening to me, as I didn't perceive any control and now, with all the control I did not know what to do with it.

I thought I'd go back to where I'd come from but couldn't, there was no behind me to search, everything was in front. I made several efforts to go behind but couldn't. I then thought of going inside self to come out the back and was immediately told, "no you cannot go there". I asked why and in a light-hearted manner the voice said, "if you did, you'd not come back".

Then the image changed to become many lines all going in different directions and where they crossed they seemed to form dense energies of differing colours. There were thousands and thousands of lines criss-crossing each other and forming a type of matrix holding these parcels of very dense differing coloured energy. It occurred to me that these parcels were objects in the physical plain.

I do not know why but this made me think of my body and I immediately found myself inside another tunnel but this had a different form to what I'd seen before. I felt it was one of my own arteries, a main one going to the heart. I saw this huge light in front of me as I followed its path. As I did, the contour of the artery changed as if it had been 'lit up' by some magic repair machine, fluff on the inside vanished and the artery became wider.

Then another change, now I'm stood on a huge gigantic ball of golden pure love. I felt I was in human form although I could not see any part of myself. It was like being on the surface of the sun but instead of emitting heat, the huge ball was emitting pure unconditional love. It had nothing other than pure love with no understanding or comprehension of anything other than love. Love was all it was.

Across to my right I could see dark patches and they seemed out of place. It was as if these areas had cooled and, although they were still part of the expanse of love, they were not aware of it. Then they arose, several of them and got bigger, like towers moving further away from the sun-like body but there was nothing to rise or go towards, just cold or lack of love.

As they did, they got darker and more rigid and then I saw the metaphor. These dark patches that had left the light now perceived themselves as separate from each other and consequently separate from the host of pure divine love.

I went towards these dark pillars and as I did, deep on their inside was the golden thread of the divine, it went up the inside of these pillars of dark. I had the feeling that these pillars had their own intent and they were focusing outward, whereas if they focused inward they would see the thread of the divine and find their way home. It was a beautiful pictorial metaphor.

I felt I was having a deeply informative experience and being shown that whatever we give our attention to is what we manifest. At this level manifestation is as easy as this. However to get there we need to address what is holding us down, our own darkness; our baggage.

Then the image began to fade and I became aware of my surroundings. I was back on the bed. It took a while before I began to re-associate and then standing up I felt totally disorientated. I couldn't associate with my legs, moving them took thought and movement was coarse. I lifted my leg high to allow it to move forward. Then I felt very nauseous, I was able to get to the bathroom before I began the purge, heaving and retching for at least five minutes and then it subsided and stopped.

Walking very carefully one step at a time, I went to the kitchen and made myself a cup of tea. I seemed to be in a half way house, neither properly connecting with the physical or having an understanding of where I'd just been or what I'd experienced, both seemed foreign. I sat quietly for a while then went outside to ground myself, where I met Rory.

Words didn't seem to want to come and what could I say anyway? I knew I was in Cusco, at Rory's retreat but that was about all I could say with any certainty. Rory led me to the grass and being barefooted, I felt the cool dampness and focused on it. I looked up, the sky was majestic, the stars, the moon, the mountains and trees. Everything was so beautiful. I felt real contentment, real connection and love for 'All That Is'.

My body seemed to float in a rhythmic dance from side to side. Rory asked if I was cold because all I had on was a t-shirt and jeans but I wasn't aware of temperature so I said no then I noticed how well wrapped up he was, it was 11.30pm and there was, to some, a chill in the air, but not to me. To me there was harmony; total love and harmony with 'All That Is'.

Someone else joined us and a conversation started but I had no interest in words, they were totally superfluous, so I went back to lie on the bed. I didn't sleep, I just was.

The following morning Rory commented on how alive I looked. He said, "Can you talk now, what was it like?" I looked at him and said, "Awesome, a lifetime of learning in a few hours that felt like weeks, beauty beyond explanation."

A little later I found Rory sat quietly looking over the Cusco valley. He said, "It seemed a deep session. I felt 'shrooms are your medicine, they're more subtle than Ayahuasca. Ayahuasca is a strong medicine that can be brutal. It is the hard lessons we need first before we move on to the subtleties of the 'shrooms." As he explained this, I recalled the first Ayahuasca session in Iquitos, when the plant told me, "you'll not find your answers here".

I hadn't needed many Ayahuasca sessions as I'd been un-conditioning myself through all the therapy I'd had in the many courses I'd taken. The regression course and the sessions revealed so much, I was already more than half prepared and hence found ease with the lessons of the 'shrooms.

It was then I recognised the differing energies of the jungle to the mountains. The jungle has a strong, course energy matched by the jungle plants. They open the mind to the wondrous capacity of consciousness, of what we really are, and in so doing begin to overwrite our Western conditioning. As we progress we explore deeper into consciousness we discover finer, more gentle, energies of the higher vibrations.

Rory explained the mountains hold the pure energy that has not been blended with the confused and darker energies of the lower lands He'd told me this before, this time I felt he was right.

The following day I recalled my experiences from the regressions at Hogwarts that now seem so long ago. Deep learning doesn't reveal it's depth until a couple of days after the experience and I now knew why. What happened to me that wonderful night with the 'shrooms was that I had my unconscious mind reprogrammed. It changed the ground rules.

My previous conditioning on which all my behaviours were controlled had been rewritten. It would take a day or so for me to understand the depth and consequences of that change as it has to get into the thinking left brain. The simplest thing I can say now is that I have discovered a new degree of acceptance, of surrender, of contentment and love for 'All That Is'.

This love can be severely tested, I still have an ego and thinking chatter, but beneath it lies a deeper understanding of the magnificence of consciousness.

I'd been in Cusco only a few weeks and what a few weeks they had been.

16 Munay Medicine

Things were looking up. I'd found an apartment in San Blas, a beautiful part of Cusco. I'd settled into a routine and discovered 'The Meeting Place', a coffee shop where, true to its name, I did meet a lot of people. I'd joined a writers group that turned out to be more of a philosophy discussion group and I enjoyed making more contacts, I was developing a social life.

It was towards the end of March when Rory told me that in about six months time he planned to move back to England. The lease on his property was due, the landlord indicating he wanted the property back. Rory had invited Maria to take over his business when he left.

Maria had found a beautiful new location in the Sacred Valley and together they asked me to join them.

I was both flattered and surprised. The thought of running a retreat hadn't occurred to me but I did so very much enjoy being with people that were discovering the medicines, especially witnessing their awe of their experiences. I found it easy to talk through their experiences and where appropriate to add complementary bits about quantum science and Buddhism, it all fitted and so naturally.

The more I thought about it, the more sense it made. My energy healing, NLP, Hypnosis and PLG background were all about helping people. The plants offered a significant shortcut in helping people understand at a deeply profound level. What also occurred to me was Otto Scharmer and *Theory U*, changing peoples mind set, lifting them to Level 4 and there is no doubt the medicines change mind sets, they help us to see through our conditioning.

I recalled my soul regression with Christine when she asked me to be taken to a life that would have significance to this one and then seeing myself as an apothecary, mixing medicines. The more I thought the more sense it all made, however it'd be a few weeks before the certainty sank home. Recording my conversation with the psychic Melinda paid massive dividends.

It seemed I was sailing on the crest of a wave. I hadn't been in Cusco two months; when we follow our intuition things become so simple.

Simple until they are not that is. Rory and Maria had a disagreement and decided they couldn't work together. I was on the outside of this and didn't know the full story and didn't want to know, this came back to bite me.

Then Rory's landlord changed his mind and offered to renew his lease thus removing Rory's need to move.

The great plans lay in ruins but it still made sense for me to be involved with a retreat. I'd had a great time with the evening discussions in Iquitos and I'd done the same a few times with Rory's guests. So even though the initial plans were in tatters, a seed had been planted in my head and it had already germinated.

Maria and I loved the Sacred Valley and the energy of Tambo del Caminante, a six bedroom, bed and breakfast-style hotel in the valley. Set in the most stunning of locations, adjacent to the Sacred River and under the gaze of the majestic and highly energetic mountain Apu Pitusiray, Tambo del Caminante was perfect.

Staying in Cusco was now less appealing. A few discussions later, Maria and I decided to continue with our plans to move to the valley. Things were though not quite as simple as Rory's experience with the plants was a significant loss, neither Maria nor I were dispensers of medicine.

We formed a new business, Munay Medicine. Munay means 'heart' in Quechua, which is the pre-Inca language still spoken in the Andean mountains of Peru. We also started detailed discussions about a three year lease with Pedro-Luis, the landlord for the Tambo but we were short of a medicine man.

<u>Munay Medicine</u>

We needed someone special. There are many people in Peru now jumping on the bandwagon of growing Western interest in the sacred plants and especially Ayahuasca. As a result, people calling themselves 'shaman' are appearing everywhere. However not all really understand the plants, the energies they create or consciousness.

A few weeks earlier, Max a 27 year old American with a light easy going energy had provided Rory with his very special liquid Wachuma and although my experience was truly difficult, I knew it was a very powerful medicine. Max had an in-depth knowledge of plant medicines, their history, active chemical components and the different experiences different combinations can provide. His explanation of the chemistry was well beyond my understanding. Rory was very impressed and called him an alchemist and he certainly is. We decided to talk to Max and we explained our plans. Happily, he agreed to join Munay Medicine so we were three, a team was forming.

Many retreats in Peru fly under the radar and do not go to the expense of registering their business with the authorities or arranging visas. We decided to be above board and do things right, however this does cause a considerable overhead and creates a sticky mess of bureaucratic red tape. It was after one of the several meetings we had with our attorney that I invited Maria to listen to the recording, then a year old, of the reading I had with Melinda. I'd listened to it a few days earlier and had forgotten some of what she said.

Melinda said: "You will be running a retreat; people will come many thousands of miles and stay with you, not for hours, for days, many days at a time". Just one of the many things Melinda said. This was for me confirmation that I was on my destined path.

Maria and I had discussed the type of retreat we wanted and it was such an easy discussion as we found there was automatic agreement.

My first Ayahuasca experience, and what an experience it was, had been without a shaman. In Iquitos a shaman was involved and in Cusco with Rory again no shaman. Maria did not want shaman involved, her perspective was it was better to have a direct connection with the plants rather than to rely on a third party, and from my experience I agreed, I found the singing a distraction.

Max was even more strongly of the same opinion and so was Rory. Rory explained that shaman only became involved after the Spanish conquest. Originally shaman would take people into the jungle, serve the medicine, leave and return hours later. This was a 'Wachuma' ceremony. The Spanish outlawed this.

The ceremonies that were acceptable to the Spanish were where a shaman was involved and the name changed from Wachuma to San Pedro. One can speculate that the Catholic influence required the route to God was only via the church and a Priest and so to experience the plants an intermediary was needed.

I felt a direct connection with the plants, experiencing them in isolation was the most profound of all my experiences. In Iquitos I discovered I was my own distraction and I now understood that although the shamans singing was beautiful it too added to the distraction. I also did not feel comfortable with dancing, rattles, feathers and smoke blown over me. Whether this is my Western conditioning or something else I do not know,

however to me it adds no value to the experience and I know
some may disagree.

17 Wachuma (San Pedro)

Wachuma is a cactus native to the Andes. It contains mescaline, which in the UK is classified as a Class A drug. Possession carries a maximum sentence of seven years imprisonment. The supply of mescaline carries a maximum sentence of life imprisonment.

If I was doing in the UK what I was now set to do in Peru, I could be locked up for life.

After the Spanish victory over the Incas in 1572, the name Wachuma was changed to San Pedro, after Saint Peter the Catholic saint. The Spanish believed San Pedro opened the gates of heaven, which it certainly does.

Wachuma does not taste nice. It is unpleasant to drink, the more often you drink it the worse it tastes, you don't get used to it, in my experience it's the opposite.

My early experiences with Wachuma were physically challenging. I would feel ill, purge and generally not enjoy myself. After a couple of days I would sense a positive shift, a feeling of wellbeing so I thought I should persevere. Wachuma is not a recreational drug it's a medicine. A ceremony would last over 24 hours, the second day bringing a sense of tranquillity, comfort and general wellbeing.

Initially, my right arm would shake violently. I could stop the shaking by focusing on my arm but as soon as I stopped focusing, the shakes would return. This continued until my fourth or fifth ceremony when I was given a black spherical crystal to hold and all the shaking stopped. However instead of the shaking, I got a vision of being a Spanish conquistador riding a horse and with a sword in my right hand slaughtering hundreds of people. This caused a lot of anger to flow through me about my behaviour, killing so many innocent women and children.

My fall off the ladder a year earlier and the damage to the arm
that killed so many now seemed very pertinent. Zak told me I
was coming back to Peru to "put things right" and the regression
to being a conquistador seemed to provide some evidence that
there were things to put right.

I've had many experiences with Wachuma, many more than with
Ayahuasca, I find it a very powerful medicine. In my experience
Ayahuasca is more visionary, more external whereas Wachuma
is more experiential, more internal. I have picked three
experiences to describe, all highly significant and two can be
seen as polar opposites.

Hand of God

In July 2015, I took Max's liquid Wachuma. There were meant to
be four of us but three dropped out, so I took it in isolation. I sat
peacefully on my own and set my intentions as healing my body
and wanting to better understand and experience the energies of
Mother Earth, Gaia or the Peruvian name Pachamama, whatever
we choose to call her. My intentions were certainly met.

I had no unpleasant physical effects, no purge or sickly feeling,
time passed and after a few hours my appreciation of the 3D was
significantly highlighted. It was like one of those viewers we had
as children that enhanced the visual 3D, like more 3D than we
normally see, everything stood out. Colours became saturated
similar to Ayahuasca, everything was enhanced as if I was now
seeing the world in extra high definition.

I could see trees in the far distance with yellow stripes that
formed geometric shapes; I could see detail so far beyond what I
normally did. It's like I had previously seen everything in low
definition 2D and suddenly it was 3D HD. The 1967 song 'I Can
See For Miles', by British rock band The Who, really sums it up.

My vision was significantly better than it had ever been. This was
coupled with a profound sense of wellbeing and total love for 'All

That Is', for nature, for trees, for plants, for animals and above all for human beings, for people. The only way I could give this experience the description it deserves would be to say I'd touched the hand of God. I can see why the Spanish believed it opened the gates to heaven.

Ian an American friend with whom I'd been in Iquitos, had described his experience as better than an orgasm and I now fully appreciate what he meant. It was joyous loving wonderment that lasted about six hours. Towards the end I saw, through sacred geometry, how everything is formed and connected.

Everything is made up from geometry and I could see it all as one, all connected three dimensionally. Something directly in front of me I could see was connected by a thin line to something else in a totally different location. Add to this the feeling of total love for everything that exists. It was the most beautiful experience.

A week later, every time I settled into a meditative state, this experience would return. The perfection of creation the most beautiful state, seeing the world and nature as it truly is. In this state, thinking is totally suspended, comfort, wellbeing and love for 'All That Is' prevail.

I discussed this with our landlord Pedro-Luis, who is a teacher of Andean Cosmology. He explained the experience in Andean Cosmology terms as entering the fifth dimension.

Pedro-Luis explained there are three elements to us, the physical, of this world, the emotional and spiritual. In Andean Cosmology terms, I had experienced the fifth dimension and once learnt it cannot be undone.

Pedro-Luis also gave descriptions from the bible, "we are in this world but not of it", is one I recall. He also explained that Wachuma works with the etheric body and why the plant is a natural source of physical healing. Coupling this with my Reiki experience of healing and I began to understand why I felt a strong connection with Wachuma. Energy healing works on the etheric body.

I felt different and meditation became a joyful quiet settlement into the true nature of 'what' we are.

Two sides to the coin

On Thursday 3 September 2015, I again had a feeling I should experience another Wachuma. My previous ceremony two days earlier had not been brilliant, the medicine worked well but there were too many people around. I found I was distracted often which considerably lessoned my experience and I felt I'd missed out.

On Saturday everyone was out so I decided to take the medicine on my own. I did have expectations, which I keep saying is wrong but regardless they were still there.

Max told me this particular medicine was not the same as when I'd touched the hand of God. The cacti were from a different location and it was likely I'd have a different experience, although no two experiences are ever the same.

I took the medicine at about 9.30am and after about three hours I got the shakes. Thinking it was possibly low blood sugar I had some fruit it made little difference. As the hours past I realised I was not going to have the experience I so wanted.

The shakes were not overly unpleasant but I'd certainly prefer not to have them, they were again all around my right arm and hand. As before I could stop them but as soon as I let my focus slip they would return. I thought I'd gone past this shaking but it was now back as strong as ever.

At around 6pm people returned to the Tambo and all I could report was the shaking. We had dinner around 7pm and afterwards I sat in the lounge in front of a large log fire with Harold, a guest opposite me.

The shaking seemed to get stronger and after trying a few things to 'shake it off', I decided to surrender to it and see just how strong it would become. Stronger it certainly became. Whereas previously, when the shakes got to a certain level, I'd intervene, this time I just relaxed and watched my right hand shake so strongly I seemed to have three hands. I could actually see three hands, one in the middle and one on either side. The shaking was the most intense it had ever had been and it became even stronger. It became so strong that I brought my hands together as if in prayer. I didn't know what else to do, I thought it may help subdue the shaking but it became more intense as my left hand and arm joined in.

At this stage I realised I'd totally lost control and even if I wanted to I was now unable to stop it. Both my arms and hands were shaking very fast and uncontrollably.

Then from the thumbs my hands parted and moved toward my face. This was not my doing, it was happening all on its own and I was becoming alarmed. I looked over toward Harold and he was looking at me with his eyes very wide open. What on earth was happening? I had no idea.

As my hands covered my face my head began to shake, so strongly it would be impossible for anyone to shake their heads so fast themselves. I thought my head would explode.

Then I stood up, my hands fell to my sides, I threw my head back and let out a strong and very loud scream.

The next thing I knew I was kneeling on the floor purging extremely deeply and very loudly. It had been less than an hour since I'd had a full meal but I was not sick, the purge seemed to come from my whole body, I felt energy rise from the very depth of my being and flood out through the mouth, right in front of the fire. There were no physical signs of a purge, just the most almighty and extremely loud retch.

This happened around five or six times and finally stopped. I sat on the floor very still physically, mentally and emotionally still. I was unable to think. I just sat frozen to the spot as if in a hypnotic trance. After a while I seemed to get my senses back, I got back on the sofa and lay down. I could not speak I was in a space of a totally silent mind.

Time passed and I finally said to Harold, "What happened?" Harold replied saying he had no idea but that whatever came out needed to.

I feel that whatever it was, a deep and powerful energy was expelled. I also feel it was not something of this dimension and possibly connected to something that had happened during my PLR course.

On the PLR course we were practicing psychic surgery using inter-dimensional travel. At one stage I had a difficult moment as I felt there was something inside of me and I became very unsettled. Andy saw I was becoming alarmed, so he intervened and stopped the exercise. Perhaps intervention then wasn't the answer. Sometimes things need to be allowed to go their full course. I certainly feel it was a very significant event and that I am better for experiencing it but what it was I have no idea.

I've since done Wachuma on many occasions and there has been no more shakes, finally I was rid of them.

Instant Psychic

In early November, Max and I went to Rory's with a new recipe Wachuma. Max experiments in ways to make Wachuma and he had discovered something new. He first tries it on himself then if he believes it to be better than previous brews, he invites others who know the medicine well, to try it. Rory and I know Max's medicines and we were both keen to try. If the feedback is good Max then offers it to clients.

We started at 9.15am but by noon I'd felt nothing. Well, something, a little like drinking half a bottle of wine. At around 1.30pm it began to take effect. It was nothing like Max's previous Wachumas, the most significant thing to me was people's faces. They were continually morphing showing different faces and expressions. The most significant was Max himself as I felt I could see what he was feeling. We just had to look at each other and there seemed a different level of understanding. Not in detail but in feeling, we both felt it and all we could do was embrace.

Sharon was one of Rory's guests who had volunteered to be a guinea pig, she was sat nearby and again her face began morphing into other faces and I got the feeling of sadness. So I asked if there was sadness within. The next three hours were fascinating.

There certainly was sadness within and a lot came out. I was so 'tuned in' to Sharon that I could feel what she was going through and my questions seemed to be channelled. On two occasions, I noticed the image of a young man I'd guess in his late twenties, he was sitting some distance away and just looking at Sharon. I didn't take much notice but he appeared again after we'd finished and then I told her someone was nearby. I described him in detail and Sharon was awestruck. She knew exactly who it was and he is still living which still does confuse me. He had a few distinctive features there could be no mistake.

Sharon said the session helped her a lot. I'd never counselled anyone whilst in the medicines. I felt it was one of the best sessions I've ever conducted.

Other uses of Wachuma

From my experience, Wachuma is an extremely powerful and healing medicine, it is being successfully used to treat post-traumatic stress and depression. If more people took it there would be less anger and hate and considerably more love and compassion in the world.

For people to be prevented from experiencing the love that Wachuma showed me is, in my opinion, a crime against humanity. That may sound strong but I feel it is a crime to stop people from having the experiences I have had from Ayahuasca, Wachuma and Magic Mushrooms. If people like myself wish to explore consciousness then they should, without the state intervening and locking them up.

Graham Hancock is right; it is a war on consciousness.

18 Still a bumpy road

In May 2015 I returned to the UK to see my family, and a nice time it was, I'd spent time with the children who are all settled with partners. Steph and I had nice meal together with perhaps a little more openness than we'd shared for a long time, it was good and we had a laugh at and with each other.

A few months earlier I'd met Ingrid, a German lady who lives in the Sacred Valley and on my return I'd arranged to rent a room from her until we could take over the Tambo. Meeting Ingrid cannot have been a coincidence as I discovered her to be fascinating and deeply wise. This was a real high and night after night we sat talking about spirituality. It was like being back at the Buddhist Society or with Owen, the only difference being there was never red wine at the Buddhist Society.

I was though still having to undergo the traumas of everyday life. You can be as spiritually connected as you can conceive but unless you are living in a cave on a hillside, you still have your life to lead and my life, was not creating for me the "lustre" that Zak had told me to expect in Peru.

Zak had told me I had changed soul groups, that I was now in a higher vibrational group and as a result I'd meet more 'higher vibrational' people. Well, it didn't feel like it.

As soon as I got back on the 20th of June I wanted a meeting with Maria and Max. What a meeting it was, the energies had changed, the vibration lowered and inside I felt very uncomfortable, my gut feelings were not good. I left the meeting feeling I'd made a mistake.

The next three months became increasingly more difficult. One bad episode followed another. On more than one occasion Max came to speak to me looking for counsel about issues he was facing with Maria. After two months Maria was hardly speaking to me and not speaking to Max at all. Finally I said to myself, very seriously, just like I had after winning GCHQ, I said, "this cannot go on." It came from deep within. Then another seemingly separate issue coincided, it explained something.

Rory's father had died and he had to return to the UK. He had a retreat booked and Tracie came down from Iquitos to stand in for him. I met Tracie in Pizac and we walked around the market together. Tracie and I immediately picked up where we'd left off some eight months earlier. I recalled just how easy conversation is with her.

Tracie is one with whom I can have deeply profound discussions about the things I love discussing. She is also a good listener and counsellor, she runs a retreat so that could be expected. I explained to Tracie the problems I was facing with Maria and asked how she thought I could better deal with them.

However Tracie explained the issues Rory had had but from his wife Anna's perspective. I was given an observational and seemingly unbiased view as to what had actually gone on. I recognised what I was experiencing was a repeating cycle.

Maria was not able to cope with team working or have the flexibility or communication skills a small team needs. Team working was my commercial background so this is where the foundations of the conflict lay. Tracie went though my options and they were limited.

I knew what I had to do and realised that if I was to be true myself I had to take on the challenge.

In early September I asked Maria to leave and at the end of the month just after the Blood Moon she did. It had been a traumatic episode as I truly hate conflict, but I knew I had to do it if Munay Medicine was to prosper.

So why, when there was to be more lustre in my life, did I go through this? I spent many hours in a hammock under the gaze of the majestic mountain Apu Pitusiray, meditating on this and the answer when it came seemed so obvious.

There is no way I'd have ever contemplated starting a retreat, it never crossed my mind. It was Rory who suggested I join him and Maria. That opened my mind to a new possibility and then Rory dropped out. Maria had found a property and an attorney so it just fell into place.

All it needed was money and Maria had none though I still had some of the proceeds from our house sale, so I provided the cash and we were away. It was after the money from the UK had arrived, and I'd returned to the Valley that energies had changed.

Things were being set up for me to ultimately take full control of Munay Medicine. Maria had played the part I needed, so now she could return to the US. We had to go through the difficulties we went through to get to the position where I was running the business, alone.

All my working life I'd worked for someone, I'd always had a boss. When we started Munay Medicine I still behaved like that, I didn't 'step up' to take control or display any authority. I didn't feel I wanted any responsibility, I'd had too much of that in my commercial career. The result was I sat back and things went astray and I reacted to the outcomes without recognising the cause, me. I should have displayed more authority and taken more control than I did.

After Maria's departure, things settled down. Max and I developed a much closer relationship and we discovered why we were not attracting the number of clients we anticipated. There was no SEO (Search Engine Optimisation) on our website home page so to search engines such as Google, we were invisible. Equally 'Retreat Guru' the marketing company that we expected would provide us with clients had the same issue. A search for our name on their site provided zero results. Again I should have known better. If I'd checked the work Maria was doing, I'd have found this.

At a spiritual level, Maria had got me to where I am. We all play our parts, sometimes big, sometimes small to bring others where they need to be. Life is very well orchestrated. I will always be grateful for the part Maria played for me in creating Munay Medicine.

So in October 2015 I was exactly where I was meant to be. Exactly where Melinda had told me I would be back in June 2014.

A few weeks after Maria left I contacted Tracie and asked her if she would join me running Munay Medicine. Tracie has been running retreats for over seven years, she would be a tremendous asset, however it would be a big step, leaving PheonixAyahuasca and the jungle of Iquitos for the Sacred Valley.

I was pleasantly surprised at her response; it was a 'definite maybe'. We continued discussing the possibilities until in early December she told me she would be returning to Australia for Christmas and would join Munay Medicine in Jan 2016 and she did. Now we had a team of team players.

19 The Collective

As things settled down at Munay, I settled down also. I'd been, as the Chinese proverb acknowledges, through interesting times. I'd had an interesting time with Wachuma, albeit I'd not always been consciously aware of the impact, I knew it was a powerful medicine. Mushrooms however were at a different level for me and I hadn't had the opportunity with mushrooms since I'd been with Rory in Cusco.

With Maria's departure, I needed a translator and put a request out on the local expats page on Facebook. Within hours I was speaking to Danny, who spoke fluent English and Spanish and lived only a mile away. We had our first meeting with the accountant and I discovered Danny grew mushrooms and I asked him if he had magic ones. He did, what a coincidence.

Danny had Philosophers Stones, which I had not experienced before. I was though about to enter the highest realm I had ever encountered. I do not know but I believe it to be the highest realm we in the 3D could ever enter. It is difficult for my mind to conceive of anything higher.

The effects came on pretty quickly. I'd say within less than an hour and they lasted about three. First there was a feeling of abandonment, detachment from all things around. I felt extremely calm with a degree of confidence that everything was perfect; I felt very comfortable. I do not know how long this lasted. I'd guess half an hour, maybe a lot longer but I surrendered to it totally. I became it, accepted it. It was a beautiful feeling I lost any sense of time and locality. I wasn't lying on a bed but floating in a sea of pure tranquillity.

Then suddenly I was home. It wasn't a thought, it was a knowing and with it a remembering of such perfection, such quality. It was a feeling of being, and that alone. I just 'was' and there was nothing else, nothing at all.

I was perfection without the need to acknowledge it, without any understanding of anything. 'I' just was. There was no thinking at all, no intellect. There was only feeling that 'I' was 'All That Is'. Nothing else existed. It was impossible to conceive of anything else as that would require thought and there wasn't any thought, just pure being.

I felt an urge run through my body and I let out the most extensive, deep and loud yell. 'I'. This was followed a few seconds later by a louder one and then again another, it reverberated through my body, I felt, I knew, I was 'All That Is'. The yell of 'I' set of a vibration that I seemed to follow. The pronunciation was not a clear 'I' it had a degree of 'high', like a mixture of the both, 'Iigh'.

The comfort is indescribable; I'd not know where to begin, other than it was pure, unconditional love, but somehow without that understanding. There was no bliss, just the extreme heightened experience of pure being.

Then I felt the collective, it had some simple imagery but it was really a feeling. This was the first time imagery had been part of the experience. It was an ever-changing connected form of shapes that I recognised. I knew it to be the collective of 'All That Is'. If I could draw these images accurately they would look pretty uninspiring. They didn't have any colour, visual beauty or complexity. In fact they didn't seem to have form. Yes, yet another seeming contradiction, I just cannot describe it. However I knew this space, I'd always known it, it was more than familiar as it was me. I knew this was home, this is where I belonged this is what I knew and what I am.

If I could have understood happiness then I was quite happy there, however this was pure feeling that cannot be translated into words.

Then I started to feel I was being pulled away. As if some giant magnet had me and it was impossible to resist and I didn't even try. I felt as if by being pulled out of the collective I was losing something. I felt I was descending and this brought the first acknowledgement of thought. It was the first recognition of separation, being apart from the collective, and that required thought. It brought with it the appreciation of distance and time. These didn't exist before.

I had no appreciation of language, I couldn't speak, I expressed a vibration; a sound like that I have heard from whales. I made a deep yearning sound as I saw all that I loved, all that I knew moving away. I also felt that the same yearning was reflected.

Then came the recognition as to why I was separating, it was instantaneous. The reason for creation, the reason for separation, my soul purpose, I knew it all in an instant. I felt myself descend more quickly, my vibration was slowing and as this happened I became aware of being David Walton, lying on my bed and immediately thinking.

It was about 11pm as I sat up trying to make order of what had happened. Trying to understand something I thought I already knew, however I was confused as two things seemed to overlap, the experience I'd just had, what I am, and the thinking about who I am and why I'm here. The thinking head caused confusion and a degree of discomfort, I couldn't just accept and I had a restless night.

The following day Max and Bianca asked me what the experience was like. I sat for a moment and contemplated how to give a quick summary. As I did I felt the energies grow within me and I let out the extremely loud "I". Max then said, "it was good then", a world ranking understatement.

It was a few days later I began to make sense of everything that has happened to me since I was five years old. It didn't come through thinking; it came as a seeming obvious observation, a feeling, a knowing that had to be thought about in order to be articulated, in order to be shared.

Thought and 'being' are different; they are incongruent. It is what I have been pondering with in so many discussions with Owen in Dubai. Being and doing, living in the moment or planning, looking forward or reflecting on the past is not mindfulness. I am not the first to recognise this and I'll not be the last, but the conundrum created by being in the 3D exists. We have mortgages, how to square that circle requires a change in how we see ourselves and how we behave.

We exist, we are. However we are locked into a paradigm that is a pure illusion, created by ego the platform that separates us from the collective, without it we'd not be separate and not be here. The obvious next question is, so why are we here?

The recognition of 'I' is recognition of what we all are, all different facets of self, of the collective, of I. The concept of God is a creation of people, of religion and no one will ever find self in religion. The concept of a God creates a fundamental separation from self, creates a higher order, something to dominate us. It's untrue, it's a belief we have been taught, it's programming, conditioning in order to subjugate us.

We have all decided to come here, to experience separation, why? What is the reason for creation? Well it's simple and more simple than many would have us believe. What I am about to describe may seem different to what I accept from *Disappearance of the Universe*, possibly, certainly on the surface. That doesn't mean *Disappearance* maybe wrong, it means that from my experience I have a different interpretation, again it is possibly due to the limitation of words to accurately describe an experience.

We, I, Us, We the collective, we are 'All That Is'. However from the perspective of what we see, hear, smell, taste, or physically feel, this part is an illusion created for the experience. However not the experience originally intended to be the world in which we find ourselves.

Creation

The intent behind creation is somewhat different to that which we are mostly experiencing. So the collective made a mistake, what! Well no, and possibly yes depending on how you interpret what I'm about to set out.

The experience of leaving the collective taught me so much and it seemed instantaneous deep and profound learning. The reason for creation is to experience self, self in many forms. It came from the moment of expressing "I". The word.

We can only learn from experience if we live the part. Hence the need for ego for separation, to enable self to truly experience what self set out to experience.

Creation was created to experience the beauties of sound, full orchestras, all music, the beauty of a solo voice, the sounds of the birds etc.

To experience the visual beauty of the mountains, valleys, lakes, fields, flowers, of art, etc. To experience the taste of different foods, of spice, sweet, salt and sour. To experience the scent of flowers, to experience touch, the feeling of objects, of others etc.

Many of these elements are created by others, but others are nothing but self. Creation is 'All That Is', our creative abilities are to be shared with us all, with the All.

This is what we chose to do. To leave the collective so we can learn the experience of the senses we have been gifted. Creation, that big bang, was to have a broader experience of 'being', of self, of I. Of all the things we can conceive, of all the things we can create.

I have pondered the difference between my experience of leaving the collective and what the disciples Thomas and

Thaddeus have explained about creation being a divine accident. At first these two interpretations seemed at odds, until meditating on this seeming contradiction I saw the answer. A billionth of a fraction of a second after the initial divine accidental thought of separation a second thought of what an experience it could be. I wonder though if I am yet to discover more to this, the most complex of all questions, 'for what purpose creation?' For now I have an answer.

In separating from the collective we also chose something special. We chose to learn something we chose a purpose, a soul purpose.

Soul Purpose

As I was descending from the collective, as thought came to me, I recognised what my soul purpose was, that being to teach, to teach what has been lost.

This confirmed everything I'd been told, from the soul regression with Christine in London, by Melinda, Nicola and Zak.

Following my intuitive to move to Cusco, going with the flow, the early discussions with Rory and Maria, how that all worked out to bring me to the Sacred Valley and how Maria's departure was all pre-destined to get me here, it seemed so obvious.

So it should be easy from hereon in. If it was all set up then success seemed to be inevitable although it wasn't feeling that way. I pondered, meditated and went deep inside self. Just what was I missing? What hadn't I yet seen?

Max, Bianca and I had sorted out the website, we'd addressed the 'Retreat Guru' marketing company issues, we had many recommends and were at the top of their site, but too few enquiries, why?

Then Rory called. Would I like to come over for an Ayahuasca session? He had a new brew and wanted Max and I to try it before he gave it to clients. I'd said yes before I'd recalled my last ceremony when Ayahuasca had said to me, "You'll not find what you are looking for here." When I was also so heartily sick of the images that wouldn't go away. I could also do Ayahuasca here at Munay Medicine but never felt inclined. However, even when I recalled all this my automatic reaction felt right.

Ayahuasca Returns

So off to Rory's I cheerfully go and had just one third of a cup of this unpleasant tasting tea. I lay down in a darkened room a little after 7pm and waited. After about an hour, Mother Ayahuasca introduced herself.

I was suddenly sitting on a sofa, in a beautifully adorned apartment, looking out of a very large panoramic window with a city below to the left and mountains to the right, I was in a very high-rise apartment block.

Then Mother Ayahuasca said, "Does this suit you better?" I laughed. I didn't get any of the images I'd had before. I did though feel a sense of comfort I hadn't had in previous Ayahuasca experiences. Nothing else seemed to happen other that the comfort got very deep and I just accepted it. After a while a man appeared, he was stood in the window.

He said, "You are looking for the universe to support you. You are asking for things but you are not connecting to the universe when you ask. How do you expect the universe to support you if you are not connected to it?"

It made perfect sense but as far as I knew I was connecting through meditation. Then a thought sprang to mind, am I doing both things together? When I meditate, I first set my intention, then get so relaxed, so calm and my thinking head switches off. I haven't set my intent or seen the outcome of what it is I needed, when I'm connected. This seemed the missing link, what I was missing.

So deep in the Ayahuasca, I started my meditation routine and as I did, then I saw the most beautiful yet simple image. It was everything all the other imagery I'd seen was plus so much more as it seemed to radiate love and in some way was hypnotic, I felt drawn towards it. As I did it opened, it was a gate, a gate made from huge crystals, red, green, blue, yellow and more. Then it just faded away. I tried to get back but it had gone. I lost the imagery and slowly returned to my conscious mind.

A while later Rory came to check on me, it was 10pm, I felt it'd been a lot more than three hours. I hadn't purged and felt wonderful. "How are you?" he asked. I didn't know how to answer, after a few seconds I said, "amazing". Rory left and a few minutes later the purge came, both ends simultaneously, quite unpleasant. One doesn't do the plants for recreation.

I didn't sleep at all that night. I lay very still and calm and enjoyed the state of just 'being', very much like a very deep meditation. My mind was blank until a thought just 'sprang in' that raised a question. If I'm following my destined path then what was this obstacle for, why do I suddenly need to do something? Then another thought, I needed time to finish my book, if Munay Medicine was full then I'd have a perfect excuse to continue procrastinating and not put the effort in. As this thought circulated my mind said very clearly to me, "Nothing will happen until you finish the book". I knew what I had to do.

I got up at 9am with a very still mind. I discussed the experience with Rory, the sense of humour Mother Ayahuasca had shown with her introduction and the answer to the question, that I hadn't asked, but the reason I was drawn to the session I am sure.

When I mentioned the gate Rory said, "it was important, that is
your future, the next time you need to take more medicine". So a
week later, I did.

This time I took half a cup, I so badly wanted to see that gate
again, to find out what lay behind it. Sadly though, I didn't get
anywhere near it. It was the least dramatic Ayahuasca
experience I've had. There was very little to describe, only one
event however it delivered a profound message.

The man from the previous ceremony was in front of me, a little
distance away but not far. He explained that where I was, in the
space Mother Ayahuasca had made for me was the only place
that was real. He explained that below, in the quagmire and
chaos of the physical plain there will be continual turmoil and
for those stuck there, that's what they will experience, time and
time again, it's their choice.

He said that we all individually have to want to lift ourselves out.
There is no gigantic shift coming to save us, no new awareness
lifting us en masse into higher dimensions, we have to do it
ourselves. If we ask for help it will be forthcoming. Then he went
and I was left once again in a very nice tranquil state.

There will not be a massive event, lifting the worthy into a
higher dimension. We individually have to take responsibility for
ourselves and this is how we will change the world in which we
live. If we were all true to ourselves then the world in which we
live would be so different.

It's our individual responsibility, no other person or event will
do it for us.

As Siobhan had said at Stonehenge;

Redemption for those that see,
Chaos for those that refuse to see and
Madness for those still battling with ego.

20 Madness

Those battling with ego control our society and we can see what they have achieved, an uneven distribution of wealth, conflicts and wars. We need look no deeper than Siobhan's statement to understand why.

It is sheer madness to deny people the experience of divine love, to deny the awareness of higher dimensions and the understanding that there is so much more to life.

It is sheer madness to prosecute and imprison people for experiencing divine love through Ayahuasca, Wachuma and Magic Mushrooms. The plants liberate people from conditioning; it greatly benefits them and ultimately the more that do will benefit society as a whole.

It is sheer madness to criminalise plant medicines whilst promoting alcohol and tobacco. Indeed those promoting tobacco plead freedom of individual choice.

It is sheer madness to deny research on the health benefits of these powerful plant medicines.

It is sheer madness to let so many suffer, with stress-related illnesses, cancers and the like that the plant medicines can help cure.

The West needs to change the way they approach plant medicines and start to appreciate them not just ban them through ignorance.

Change is on the horizon

According to the British businessman Sir Richard Branson, best known as the founder of Virgin Group, which comprises more than 400 companies, things are beginning to change.

<u>Richard Branson - Finally a change in course on drug policy</u>

On the above link to Branson's own website, he discusses an unreleased statement circulated to the BBC, himself and others, from the United Nations Office on Drugs and Crime (UNODC), which has shaped much of global drug policy for decades. It calls on governments around the world to decriminalise drug use and possession for personal consumption for all drugs.

This is a refreshing shift that could go a long way to finally end the needless criminalisation of millions of people around the world. However governments have to implement it and there is resistance.

<u>Richard Branson - Time to end the war on drugs</u>

This second link relates to Portugal's very impressive and successful outcome to the decriminalisation of drugs. Ten years ago the Portuguese Government responded to widespread public concern over drugs by rejecting a war on drugs approach and instead decriminalized drug possession and use. It further rebuffed convention by placing the responsibility for decreasing drug demand as well as managing dependency under the Ministry of Health rather than the Ministry of Justice. With this, the official response towards drug-dependent persons shifted from viewing them as criminals to treating them as patients.

The evidence from Portugal is powerful;

- Drug use by Portugal's teens has declined.
- New HIV infections fell by 17 percent
- Portugal now has the lowest rate of marijuana use in the European Union.
- Drug use at colleges fell from 14.1 to 10.6 per cent.
- Heroin use for 16-18 year olds fell from 2.5 to 1.8 per cent.

- People on treatment for drug addiction rose from 6,040 to 14,877.
- Property theft dropped dramatically.

This last point, that property theft dropped dramatically, does not address the consequential impact. The reduced stress on homeowners, reduction in insurance claims and subsequent insurance costs and the saving in police time and costs. The evidence is stark.

> "Portugal's 10 year experiment shows clearly that enough is enough. It is time to end the war on drugs worldwide. We must stop criminalising drug users. Health and treatment should be offered to drug users not prison. Bad drugs policies affect literally hundreds of thousands of individuals and communities across the world. We need to provide medical help to those that have problematic use not criminal retribution".
>
> Richard Branson

Medicines not drugs

The sacred plants are not drugs, albeit they are classified as such, they are medicines. As medicines and as Portugal have done, they should fall within the jurisdiction of health ministries, not the criminal justice system.

Natural plant medicines can help heal our society, help heal the West by re-introducing us to ourselves, to spirit, to source. In so doing we will become considerably happier individually and collectively. We will see ourselves for what we really are rather than counting how much money we have.

People experiencing plant medicines will recognise materialism for what it is, they would become more supportive of each other and consequently considerably happier.

If wellbeing of the electorate was really a government priority then why are they so freighted of psychedelic medicines?

21 Reflection and progression

I feel I've come along way since I was that five-year-old terrified of my invisible boulder. I guess that's to be expected, as I'm now over 60. That said, that first experience of my boulder is still so vivid in my mind that it could have been yesterday, as could its full introduction some 43 years later.

Being one with the universe created my first change of direction, only slightly, but it changed me, it changed what I knew, how I thought, how I felt and how I behaved. It may have been only a slight change of direction just a few degrees but 12 years later it was sufficient to create such a distance between Steph and I we divorced.

Our divorce was another change but this time more significant. Once I'd got through the pain, it allowed me the freedom to discover 'what' I am rather than the 'who' I'd become living in the Western paradigm. Steph's action was the greatest act of unconditional love I feel I have ever been shown. I feel total unconditional love for her and always will.

My Nirvana experience in Paris with Zulf and Mike gave me another dose of knowing, rather than believing or understanding, that there is so much more to life. It took me nearly 10 years to fully understand the depth of that lesson. Nothing is all that there is. Nothing is the reality and it comes with such presence, refinement and quality. Something, anything that can be defined is an illusion. It is difficult to understand this, conditioned as we are into our Western tradition of object driven science.

On David Hawkins' Map of Consciousness Nirvana is at least 600 and once experienced it cannot be forgotten or the learning undone. For all my later experiences with the plants, and even considering my connection with the collective, I feel Nirvana taught me more than any other single experience. My bubble of knowing expanded so much, the unknown becoming huge.

I was beginning to understand consciousness from a different perspective, the soul and past life regressions opened yet another door. Behind this door lay a new understanding, the power of regression therapy cannot be over estimated. I learnt so much more than I have described. We all have more history than we can imagine and it controls so much of our behaviours. With this understanding the unknown became truly immense.

As my thinking logical head was pulling me back into the commercial world, I was provided with a hefty smack and my third change of direction. This was the most significant of all the changes I've been through. Falling off the ladder had an even bigger impact on my life than that of my divorce. This was a direct intervention from 'them upstairs'. My free will had been overturned and I was pointed towards Peru.

When I met the sacred plants, I was 60 and approaching them with an appreciation of consciousness through my time at the Buddhist Society and all the experiences I've had. The plants were able to take me further, faster and they certainly have. It is strange to think that, less than two years earlier, I was in a Level 1 box as regards plant medicines. How things can change when you are open to the possibility of being wrong.

The plants are very special but not a magic bullet. They show us what we're capable of experiencing, the higher realms of consciousness that it'd take years of dedicated meditation to otherwise achieve. We have to decide to leave our conditioning behind, to look deeply inside self in order to truly benefit.

Of all my plant experiences, the collective was the most significant and awesome. It was a few weeks after this experience whilst meditating on the bank of the Sacred River that the reason I had to go to Stonehenge just flowed into my mind. I needed the grounding of groundings in order to remain centred and let me connect as high as I did, to the collective. Without meeting Siobhan, I'd not be capable of going so high.

On Hawkins Map of Consciousness, the collective is in the 700 – 1000 bracket. Connecting with it came the recognition of 'I', of self. So much more came with it that is impossible to describe fully as any description is limited to that description. The collective is everything that is, the material world does not register, it is less than irrelevant, it is an illusion.

Reality does not exist in the thinking, clever logical heads. Reality exists in feeling, of knowing of the All. It's beyond our understanding in the physical dimension, certainly beyond my ability to adequately explain.

Living as we do within the 3D I do not believe it is possible to appreciate the full nature of consciousness, of the All. However as we begin our journey to the appreciation of what we are, rather than who we're conditioned to believe we are, then we will begin to improve our experience of life.

Mother earth is the greatest classroom imaginable, it is where the curriculum is designed specifically around the individual, around you, around what you chose to learn and it's experiential learning. The difficulty we face is being distracted by ego and the Western paradigm.

I do not have all the answers, indeed I have very few. What few I do have are my answers, not yours. Only you can find your answers, your curriculum is different to mine, you set a different soul purpose, different learning objectives.

Improving our experience of life.

Living in the world of thinking, doing and working hard, when we are measured by academic achievement and measure ourselves by money and assets then we're measuring an illusion. All measurement is false.

You can be wealthy and famous with a brilliant sense of humour, with many people wishing to be in your company, yet inside still so desperately unhappy. Robbie Williams taught us so much. His sacrifice is a true international beacon to what the West has become. What you may see in others is not what they see in themselves.

Although it may not seem it, there are no greener pastures other than the one you are in. The one you are in is your design, it is your pasture and it contains all you need. All you have to do is recognise what you designed and that's your purpose for being, your soul purpose. When you do this the stresses and strains you're creating will evaporate and you will see life for what it really is.

So let's make it the greenest of green pastures. This is done by looking inside at oneself and not outside at others. We are not victims of circumstance. The universe is guiding our way, it does so by being a mirror, and so we can see ourselves and see our own behaviour as the reflection shown to us by others. Do not blame, recognise.

To lift our vibration we must take 100 per cent responsibility for our own lives. Forgive everything. Holding any form of grudge is a weight, it's baggage; it holds us down. On the Map of Consciousness, blame is a lowly 30 and linked to guilt. If you blame someone, if you hold anger or resentment, then you are suppressing something inside of yourself, your own fears, guilt or shame. Remember that we are one, blaming someone else is blaming oneself. This is probably the hardest thing for a Western educated mind to understand, but it is fundamental to lifting our vibration above madness, through the resulting chaos and into the utter joy of redemption.

The response to hurt is love. Feel it, acknowledge it, be it. Only you will suffer if you don't as holding onto negative energies harms the body, ultimately despite your suppression this negative energy will emerge. Suppression of negative energies will show itself in your behaviour and ultimately your health.

Be your truth, respond to your intuition and follow your excitement. Do what you like doing, not what you think is the best for you, not what you are told is best for you, do what you feel is best for you, what you'd enjoy the most. Be true to self, totally, become fully aligned with your higher self.

Another difficult thing for a Western mind to accept is one of the most important things we need to learn, which is; *'living in the moment'*. Living in the now is key.

Living in the past and focusing on old hurts or what could have been is pointless it harms you. Forgive everything, it was learning and offer love in gratitude.

Living in the future thinking on something that hasn't happened and will not unfold as you think anyhow is equally fruitless.

I can still fall down this particular trap. Forgiving the past is effortless; I've let everything go. Not thinking about the future however is considerably more difficult, especially if there is worry and anxiety about the future. When I notice that I'm doing exactly what I tell others they should not, then I meditate. I set my intent, asking for guidance and then start the meditation set out below.

Meditation turns the thinking head off, just for a while, to give yourself the space to listen at Level 5. There are other things you can do such as walking, gardening, yoga, physical and exercise. These things give you the space you need to resolve the issues being faced as solutions and options will arise from a quiet mind. The issues facing us in the future may seem insurmountable, until a solution 'springs to mind'.

Trusting and having the courage to follow your intuition will bring its rewards. What a lesson Steph taught me. It was obviously not my intention to split up, it was hers but it has enabled me to learn more than I could ever have imagined.

Unknowingly we all work for each other, for everyone. Those that teach us the biggest lessons are our true guides, however painful the lesson may feel at the time they are angels.

Look for repeating cycles in your life. The universe, your higher self, will keep offering you same lesson until you see the reason for it; until you see what you have to learn. Once learnt then there is no need to go through it once more, it's done, you can move on.

There will come a time, likely very soon after you have finished this book, when the first opportunity will arise for you to change the way you respond to a person or an event. You will recognise your truth. This doesn't mean you have a licence to hurt someone. Honesty without tact is detrimental but recognise your truth and live it.

After the first there will be others. Rome wasn't built in a day. These small changes will, in time, be significant and you will see life through clearer filters.

Yes sometimes there will be consequences, yes sometimes upheaval but if you know it to be right, do it. Living in a stressful situation can be considered easier than the alternative, you don't know this, you think it.

What if you are not sure, not certain what will make you happy? FUD (Fear, Uncertainty and Doubt) is the biggest weapon of the ego. It creates lack of action and maintains the status quo.

> "Doubt is 100 per cent trust in a belief you don't prefer."
>
> Bashar
> Channelled by Darryl Anka

Meditation

Meditation gets through FUD as it gives the space in the mind, the space to listen at Level 5. There are many meditation techniques. I use one that works for me, there are others so if what I explain here doesn't work for you, then find another, there are many books, CDs and meditation classes available.

There are two forms of meditation, attention-focused and open-minded. Attention-focused is self-explanatory, it is what its name suggests in that you focus on something. This single focus of your attention could be a flower or a vase, or it could be someone's voice in a guided meditation. All of these are distraction techniques. Distracting the mind in order to make it stop thinking.

Open-minded meditation begins when you can quieten the mind and stop thinking without a distraction. I have taught it using a headset that measures the Gamma, Beta, Alpha, Theta and Delta brainwaves and I record a client session. From a visual representation on my computer, I can see the amplitude of the brainwaves, which reveals how the client is progressing.

Most importantly though, it enables the client to recognise what they need to do to achieve the objective of producing Theta and Delta brainwaves. By practising this daily, they can monitor their own progress and become more familiar with what works for them. In this way, a person quickly becomes an experienced meditator.

I was originally taught meditation at the Buddhist Society and initially found it so much easier to meditate in a group rather than practising in solitude. Now I can happily do both and I really enjoy guiding a meditation class. However if you are new to the practice then I'd suggest initially either getting a headset (I use a Bluetooth Mindwave) or going to a meditation class. Once you've got the hang of it, you'll discover it is really easy and a lovely experience. That said, you probably do it already without recognising it as meditation.

Most people meditate without realising it. Obviously not sat cross-legged with a straight back and eyes partially or fully closed. You don't need to meditate this way although after a while you may.

You can meditate in a queue at the supermarket, sat in your car at traffic lights, (you will likely hear a horn when the lights have changed and you haven't moved) or while you're doing the dishes. You can meditate literally anywhere. It doesn't have to be 20 minutes, it can be 20 seconds or less.

Have you ever been watching TV when your mind has just gone blank? Nothing but stillness prevails until someone asks, "Where were you?" but you can't answer because you haven't a clue. This is when the thinking mind has gone to sleep, it's a form of meditation.

Have you ever been driving and suddenly wondered how you got to where you are? You have no memory of driving those last few miles and you wonder if you had been safe? There are those that say when driving you need to concentrate 100 per cent and I'd not argue the point. However when the thinking mind turns itself off, I'd suggest you are driving more safely than when you are thinking. Just consider this, if you're not thinking then what is driving the car? It's your unconscious and it has 360-degree awareness as well as the prime objective of protecting you. It has a deeper understanding of your surroundings and that of others driving their cars, pedestrians, etc. You will recognise this when you suddenly feel the car braking before you consciously recognise why.

These are times that you are more connected to your higher self and more open to the messages. You think that you've had a blinding flash of inspiration, do you really think it was you? Well, yes it was you in one sense but it was not the thinking you, it was the Level 5 listening intuitive you.

Meditation is just stopping the thinking and giving you the space to open yourself to Level 5 listening.

The issue most have when they start meditating is the thinking head will not shut up. I'm very familiar with this and it was being in a group at the Buddhist Society that helped me overcome it. For some the first step in the technique below is not easy, conquer it and you're well on your way.

An Inca meditation and energy cleansing technique

I use and teach this meditation practice. I find it a very powerful method to start dealing with issues I may be struggling with.

Find a quiet spot, outside is preferable, sitting under a tree is nice, however sat cross legged on a lawn or in a park is just fine. Find a spot you feel comfortable in, one that feels right. It can be done in a sitting room or sat on your bed. If you can sit cross-legged with your back straight it'd help. Doing it is more important than the location.

1. Focus on the breath, on your breathing, breathing slowly in and out through the nose. This is always a good thing to do if ever you find yourself stressed or cannot sleep. In this instance, it is just to slow things down. If you're thinking about your breathing you're not thinking about anything else. After a while when you recognise you have stopped thinking you are ready to begin.

   There is no hurry no one is timing you. If you find it difficult to stop the thinking, as many initially do, then this can help.

- Follow the breath, start at the nostrils and notice a slight cooling as the air flows up the nose. Once you recognise that then;
- Notice the cooling of the bead at the inside corner of your eyes. This is a very subtle feeling so don't give up if you don't feel it straight away. Spending an hour doing this is fine.
- Once you have noticed that, then follow the breath down the back of your throat. Take your time, notice each step before you start the next one.
- Now feel the cooling of your lungs as the air fills them.

The feelings are very subtle continue this exercise until you achieve it. This first stage is very important; it's the foundation of meditation. If it takes weeks it doesn't matter, you have plenty of time. As I said, joining a meditation class can also be very helpful. The point here is if it doesn't seem to work, don't give up, persevere, for some this is the biggest of hurdles, get this right and the rest is easy, so it's well worth practicing.

When I achieve a totally quite mind I tend to just maintain it. The majority of my meditations stop here. I find answers will arise when the time is right.

However there is more that can be done with meditation. If you want to heal your body Deepak Chopra's *Quantum Healing* is a fantastic way to begin.

Following the next steps below will provide real benefit and what Janet taught us at Hogwarts.

2. Say out loud, "unconscious mind, open my root chakra and connect me to an earth energy point". Then visualise or feel a beam of light going from the base of your spine to the centre of the earth. Focus on this for a moment, feel it running down your back, straight to the centre of the earth.

3. Say out loud, "unconscious mind, open my crown chakra and connect me to the spirit realm". Visualise or feel a beam of light going from your crown straight to the heavens. Focus on it for a moment, feel it running up your back straight up into the sky and above.

4. If you haven't already, connect these two beams – one reaching down and one reaching upwards. See or feel yourself in the middle, the connection between the spirit realm and mother earth, Gaia. This is what we are in the 3D, the connection between the physical, mother earth from where everything is manifest, and the higher realms. We are both physical and spiritual beings we are multi-dimensional. Feel yourself in the middle because that is exactly where we are.

5. Now ask your guides and mother earth to remove any energies that are not serving you, not serving your soul purpose. They can take these energies up or down depending on where they are best dealt with. Now visualise or feel a swirling energy within your chest. As it swirls faster it elongates and gets thinner. The top of the elongation goes up the beam of light to the heavens, and the bottom down to mother earth. This continues until all that's left is a pencil-thin beam that you cut in half. The ends disappearing up and down respectively. Take your time with this; play with it.

6. Now ask the guides and mother earth to replace the energies you have given up with pure love. Some will come up from mother earth, some down from the heavens. You may imagine different colours, or vibration, it doesn't matter, just visualise or feel the energies coming into you and meeting at the heart. Let your heart mix these beautiful energies.

7. Let it fill your body until it overflows over your crown and out of your root chakra and the overflowing energies cover your body and unite at your chest.

You may need to do this a few times before you feel natural with it. Again it doesn't matter how many times or how long it takes, there is no time limit and no test.

See or feel the energy around you as protection, as a shell, on the outside a mirrored shell that will protect you from any negativity that may come at you from elsewhere. Say 'thank you' to the guides and mother earth. Ask your unconscious to close the root and crown chakras, (at this stage it is better to close them).

When you feel you have mastered this technique or done it several times so you feel comfortable with it you can move on.

8. Before you ask for your crown and root chakras to be closed ask your unconscious mind to open your heart chakra. See or feel the beams of light from above and below joining at the heart and direct the energy from your heart to the heart of someone that needs love. Feel unconditional love for them and send it. Once you have made that connection feel that person come towards you, as if attracted by the beam. As they get closer invite them into your heart. We are all one and that's where they belong.

    This is remote energy healing. It comes from your etheric body to that of the recipient. Recognise though, the person receiving it will be dealing with their own issues so have no expectations.

    Alternatively, you may want to direct this energy at someone you have fallen out with or a relationship you'd like to heal. This will lift your vibration as involves both forgiveness and love. Remember it must be totally unconditional love you feel for them, don't expect the phone to ring.

    You can think of healing all with waves of love emanating from your heart centre and radiating out 360 degrees around you like the ripples from a stone thrown into a pond. These ripples go around the earth. There is infinite power from above and below we are purely the conduits with the intent. Intent is our power. Send love to 'All That Is', it will be reflected.

This is very powerful. Doing it in groups is incredible so you could form a new meditation group with your friends. It's great to have a group all starting together, at the same stage learning from each other. Listen to guided meditation CDs and afterwards discuss how it worked and what you experienced. It'd be a new social circle with a common aim. Leave the wine until afterwards though.

Recall the research of Dr David Hawkins, one person thinking a loving thought outweighs that of 750,000 having a fearful thought. If there are four people meditating on love for all, that covers three million living with fear. Do that for 20 minutes and you then deserve that glass of wine, as although you will not recognise it, you will have made a difference.

9. You will feel when it's time to stop and close the chakras. Say 'thank you' to above and below.

When in that supermarket queue, or any queue that is not moving, just do the breathing and if you have time, connect yourself above and below and get rid of the negative energies that are causing frustration. It works!

There is a further development of this technique that addresses the concept of separation. We are all one so how can we have above and below?

The diagram below from the HeartMath Research Centre is a single helix toroid, I imagine the energies going much higher and lower but this is a good representation.

We are in the middle of an energy toroid, there is no separation; we are all one. If you feel the need you can fold the energies back and be the centre. Feel this, be it and bring it into your everyday life. Just a few minutes every day, just be it.

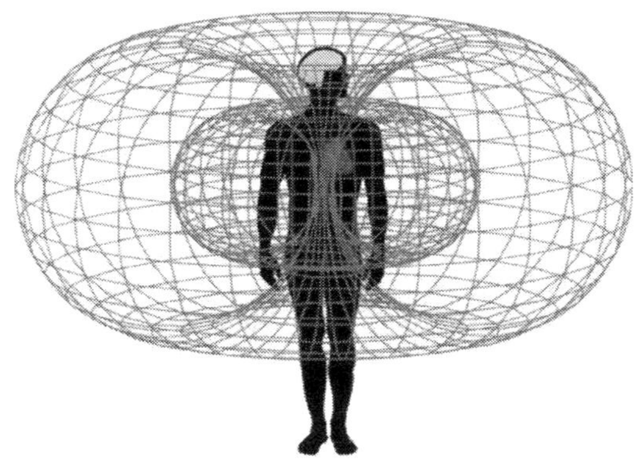

It is said by some that you need permission to direct healing to others, I don't feel so if you are directing pure unconditional love. If they don't accept it, then the love will find somewhere that does.

Saying things out loud rather than saying things silently to oneself is important as it sets the vibration for the universe to recognise. It may be suggested that as we are energy beings with intent we don't need to verbally express. My GCHQ and Maria expressions were internal but the energy within them was immense, I felt it strongly. Verbal expression is important if you're not carrying that intense level of feeling as I then was. However when you express it, you must also feel it.

The more you practice the easier and more natural it becomes and with that come the greatest benefits. Don't expect an immediate response; don't expect anything. However, be open to the possibility and when it does come, just give thanks.

Do this meditation as often as is practical. The situations we find ourselves in may have taken years of conditioning so don't expect miracles. Don't expect sudden enlightenment about what to do next. The shifts will probably be small but in time they will take you in a different direction. It's one step at a time.

If you can spend 15 minutes a day just focusing on the breath it will be hugely beneficial. If you can spend another 15 minutes meditating you will lift your vibration and begin to reap the rewards sooner. The fastest progress will come by forgiving everything and everyone and that includes you.

Manifestation

In the beginning of this book I wrote about how easy it is to manifest your desires. The number one thing is aligning with your soul purpose, I cannot stress this enough. You originally set your soul purpose, what you came to learn. You did it for a reason. Then parents, school and Western societies values taught you something else, a Western 'thinking' alternative. Are you living that alternative and wondering why you feel things are not working out, why you're not living the dream? If so, is it any wonder?

The majority of people want to manifest huge amounts of money. This is purely Western materialism and I can assure you the universe is not interested in sustaining Western materialism, it's madness.

Do you believe a Western thinking alternative should be delivered? Your soul purpose is what the universe wants to deliver, is ready to deliver, all you have to do is follow it.

Do you feel this is right or wrong? Behind all the thinking, what is your gut telling you, what are you feeling, what do you know?

If your intent is to follow your soul purpose, then how successful will your manifestation be?

In order to manifest do the meditation I explain above but after step 6, now from the heart chakra, see your future, feel it, all in the now, as if it's happened already. The thing is though, if you are following your soul purpose, your excitement, you'll not need to, it'll already be happening.

You, I, We, are One, supporting each other in ways we cannot imagine. Our conditioning, our thinking heads, our free will, our ego is a distraction, it gets in the way of the beautiful experience that living on mother earth can be.

Becoming true to oneself will show this to you. Being true to others, or believing you are being true to others by letting them lead your life, will leave you feeling empty, unhappy, cheated, resentful... or a number of other negative emotions. Time is an illusion, you have no history, there is only you in the now so forgive yourself for everything and move on.

There is more to life if you choose there to be. Only you can take the step, no one can do it for you, it is your choice and your choice alone.

If you ask for help it will be forthcoming, your higher self, the collective have infinite love and patience to help you re-discover what you are.

You are perfection, you are pure love and part of 'All That Is'. There is nothing higher than you, nothing. Believe it, be true to what you really are, part of 'All That Is'.

Once you have recognised, truly recognise this then this recognition leads you on another path, a new journey to the discovery that there is so much more to life.

You start your journey by simply being true to yourself and in so doing create your new beginning your 'new book'. This will be the beginning of making your life the beautiful experience it is meant to be.

It is down to you and you alone to decide to write it.

Appendices

1 List of video's & websites

The Lord Admiral on Bentwaters (7 minutes)

Do Schools Kill Creativity? | Sir Ken Robinson | TED Talks (20 minutes)

Changing Education Paradigms (11 minutes) – The most watched TED Talk

TEDxNASA - Dr. Sue Morter (18 minutes)

Dr Quantum - Flatland (5 minutes)

David Hawkins explains the Scale of Consciousness

Stroke of insight - Jill Bolte Taylor (18 minutes)

Our Roots Kenya

Graham Hancock - The War on Consciousness BANNED TED TALK (18 minutes)

Bashar - Ayahuasca (6 minutes)

Prof David Nutt: Putting Neuroscience at the Centre of Drug Policy (54 minutes)

www.maps.org

Psychedelic Times

Rupert Sheldrake The morphogenetic Universe (1 hour 20 minutes)

Munay Medicine

Dr Quantum - Double Slit Experiment (5 minutes)

Bruce Lipton - The New Biology - Where Mind and Matter Meet 1 of 2 (1 hour)

Bruce Lipton The New Biology Where Mind and Matter Meet 2 of 2 (1 ½ hours)

2 Books referenced

Quantum Healing – Deepak Chopra

A Lawyer Presents the Case for the Afterlife - Victor and Wendy Zamitt

Theory U (2009) - Otto Scharmer

The Case for Reincarnation – Joe Fisher

The Science Delusion – Dr Rupert Sheldrake

Living Magically - Gill Edwards

Power vs Force - David Hawkins

A Stroke of Insight - Dr Jill Bolte Taylor

What the 'Bleep" do we know – DVD

Transformed by the Light - Cherie Southerland

Divine Matrix - Gregg Braden

Journey of the Souls - Michael Newton

Silences in NGO Disclosures – Issa G Shivij

3 Sapo / Kambo frog medicine

Sapo or Kambô: Scientific Research and Healing Treatments
by Giovanni Lattanzi – lattanzi18@gmail.com (Article translated
from Spanish and edited from the original)

'Kambô', 'campu', 'sapo', 'vacino da floresta.' These are all names
for the waxy secretion of a tree frog living in the north-western
part of the Amazon rainforest (in Colombia and on the border
between Peru and Brazil). The scientific name for this frog is
'Phyllomedusa bicolor' or 'Giant Monkey frog'. In this article, I
will use the name 'Kambô.' Originally, 53 tribes used this
secretion but now only 13 small tribes still use it. It is used to get
rid of 'panema', the name they give to bad luck, as well as for
'hunting magic' and as a powerful medicine against snake bites,
malaria, yellow fever and other epidemic diseases.

Scientific research on kambô: Nine powerful bio-active peptides.
Scientific research on the secretion of this frog started in the
1980's. Nominated for the Nobel prize, Italian scientist Vittorio
Erspamer of the University of Rome wrote that this secretion
contains a 'fantastic chemical cocktail with potential medical
applications, unequalled by any other amphibian' (1). 'Among
the several dozen peptides found in kambô, up to 7% are bio-
active.'(1) They bind with receptor sites situated in the brain,
triggering chemical reactions in the human body. So far,
researchers have found nine bio-active peptides that have a
potent effect on the gastrointestinal muscles, gastric and
pancreatic secretions, blood circulation, and on the stimulation
of the adrenal cortex and pituitary gland.
Sapo / Kambo Frog Poison Being Applied by Mark Thornberry

'Phyllomedusin strongly affects intestines, bowels and
contributes to deep purging. Phyllokinin and phyllomedusin are
potent vessel dilators, increasing the permeability of the blood-
brain barrier. This facilitates access to the brain of these two, as
well as the other active peptides. Caerulein and sauvagine cause

a fall in blood pressure accompanied by tachycardia. They stimulate the adrenal cortex and the pituitary gland, contributing to heightened sensory perception and increased stamina. Both of these peptides have a strong analgesic effect, enhance endurance, increase physical strength and in general, enhance the capacity to face pain and stressful situations. They possess medical potential as digestive aids, and have demonstrated analgesic effects for those with renal colic, pain due to peripheral vascular insufficiency and cancer pain. Dermorphin and deltorphin are potent opioid peptides 4000 times stronger than morphine and 40 times stronger than endogenic b-endorphines. (1).

In the 1990's, a new peptide, adenoregulin, was discovered by John Daly's team at the National Institute of Health in the USA. Adenoregulinworks in the human body through the adenosine receptors, a fundamental component in all human cell fuel. These receptors can offer a target for treating depression, stroke seizures and cognitive loss ailments such as Alzheimer's disease. Scientific research on the peptides of kambô are opening up new perspectives on how the human brain works. The properties of kambô peptides cover a wide range of potential medical uses: treatment of brain diseases such as Alzheimer's and Parkinson's, depression, migraines, blood circulation problems, vascular insufficiency, organ diseases, skin and eyes issues, fertility problems in women and men, AID's, hepatitis, cancer, etc.

Other interesting medicinal properties of this secretion are its anti-inflammatory effects, its capacity to destroy microbes and viruses and heal infections. (1) Due to the presence of these nine peptides, kambô is one of the strongest natural antibiotics and anaesthetics found in the world and one of the strongest, natural ways to empower our immune system. The kambô treatments have short and long term effects. 'Short term, the effects are a state of alertness, good mood, enhanced resistance to tiredness, hunger and thirst' (1), the capacity to easily concentrate and focus, and a still mind which can last for several days or weeks. Long term, kambô empowers the immune system, overcomes fatigue and improves one's state of health.

With kambô, we have the opportunity to wake up the body to its full natural potential. The people who regularly receive this 'vaccine' do not get sick and have plenty of energy. Restoring a natural balance, it prevents the onset of complaints induced by viruses. Even cancer does not have a chance to grow, in some cases. For the best results, it is advisable to receive kambô regularly. In the case of heavy diseases, 2 addictions or accumulated toxins from pharmaceutical medicines, it may be helpful to double the treatments for awhile. In this way, the cleansing effects of the kambô treatments will build on one another and will last longer.

During a treatment, kambô immediately scans a person's energy field and starts to work exactly where it is needed. The process is different for everyone and the course of treatment should be planned accordingly. I have witnessed some people getting healed in one treatment, especially those with eye or ear problems. For people with addictions, results can also happen fast. Complicated cases may take longer. We may call this frog secretion a medicine, but it doesn't actually work as a typical medicine nor as a drug. It simply wakes up the body's organs, endocrine system and defence systems to their natural functions.

The day after Sapo / Kambo Frog Poison Purge;
How the indigenous tribes of the Amazon do it.
'Although difficult, the frogs can be found on the trees when they are singing, announcing the rain. The tribe members traditionally harvest the frog at dawn, also singing.'(2) In some traditions only the shaman crops the frog. The frogs are extremely poisonous and don't react when captured because they don't have any natural predators in the forest. They are actually hard to swallow, and if a snake tries, it desperately spits them out.

To harvest the secretion from the frog's skin, the frog is stretched by strings tied to its limbs into the shape of an X. As uncomfortable as it may look, the frog is not harmed during this process, and is released afterwards in perfect health. The secretion is crystallized onto wooden sticks and can later be prepared for use by mixing the dried secretion with a few drops of water.

The 'medicine' is applied by burning tiny holes in the skin with the tip of a glowing stick. The effect is immediate, as it runs in the body through the lymphatic system. The body becomes warm and the heart beats faster than normal until the person vomits the water they had been drinking in advance. All this lasts about 15-20 minutes.

Kambô, as well as other native medicines, is based on the principle of the transmission of energy from the shaman to the person who receives the treatment. The indigenous people know different ways to give this vaccine and every tribe has developed different rituals. The Katukina and the Matses tribes take kambô burns several times a night before hunting. The number of burns, the frequency of the treatments and the intention varies in each tribe. The main reason to take kambô is to remove 'panema', which is translated as bad luck, depression, laziness, sadness, or a condition attracting difficulties and disease. When nothing is going right then it is the right moment to take kambô, according to the tribes. In some tribes, kambô is also used as a tool for the young, to teach them discipline.

According to the indigenous people, kambô is first and foremost a Spirit of the forest who is to be treated with respect. Harming the frog could offend the animal and result in severe misfortune. The Matses combine kambô with nu-nu, a snuff which informs the hunter through visions of when and where prey will offer itself. The tribal members say that shamans see the frog in their visions and dialogue with it.

Many changes have happened in the Amazon during the last century from when city people moved to the rainforest to work in the rubber factories. For some years now, kambô has been used outside of the Amazon rainforest and is no longer the exclusive realm of the native tribes. New uses for kambô have come about as people who were taught by the natives started using it outside of the native tribal culture.

One of the pioneers who brought kambô to the cities was Francisco Gomes (or Shiban), who lived with the Katukina. Francisco Gomes was a caboclo, someone of mixed descent, part white and part native. His son, Genildo Gomes, founded an association cantered around kambô in the Jurua region of Brazil in 2002, called AJUREMA. There are different philosophies among those who administer kambô, particularly between the Katukina and the caboclos. The caboclos set more rules and restrictions in order to make 3 kambô treatments safe for people who are less strong than the native people and might take this medicine for other reasons than for hunting or healing malaria. Some of the restrictions include not giving this medicine to people with heavy heart problems, to pregnant women in their first trimester and to children under ten years old.

For the caboclos, the basic treatment is three doses, given at intervals of time which depend on the capacity of the person to take kambô. According to this method, the interval between two treatments should be a maximum of 28 days, or one moon. Longer than that, then the kambô will have to do all its work all over again.

During this three month treatment the treated person gets an increasing amount of points (5-7-9). The Katukinas ingest from three to five litters of a corn soup during the night before the treatment, while the caboclos drink about two liters of water a few minutes before the application. Both the Katukina and the caboclos require that one avoids solid food and salt at least 12 hours before the treatment.

Spiritual aspects;
In his article, "Kambô, the Spirit of the Shaman," Marcelo Gomes writes that kambô 'establishes a chakra realignment, a mark for

organic and psychological reorganization, from which the person changes their patterns of health'(6). Kambô is a fire medicine. When combined with the water that is drunk before the treatment, an alchemical transformation happens and old toxins are released through vomiting or urgent defecation. This cleansing process works not only on a physical level but also on a spiritual one. The frog, connecting us with our natural wisdom, mirrors our negative habits, showing us what we should avoid and what we could do in order to improve our condition.

During the kambô treatments, we receive insights. The messages given by the kambô can be very simple. Once I received a message about how poisonous the decaffeinated coffee was which I had drunk just before my kambô treatment. A friend of mine recognized a pattern in himself that he never saw clearly before. Whenever he faced an uncomfortable emotion, he would become restless and cover his unpleasant feelings with activity. After getting a few kambô treatments, he recognized this behavioral pattern and now, is better able to embrace his feelings and calm down.

Kambô unfolds the changes we need to make, in an effortless, natural way. Many of us think, 'I want to be better', 'I want to stop smoking,' etc. When we try to reach a certain result with our willpower, we are actually fighting. We've done so for many generations. With kambô, a natural wisdom is taking over our healing process. We know without thinking what we have to do or not to do in a certain situation. We become able to drop unhealthy habits and fixed ideas. In my experience, ideas are often the main obstacle, blocking us from our healing. Kambô affords us the energy we usually don't have but that we need for our spiritual path. Removing the cloud of 'panema' around our energy field, we become more open to receive from Spirit.

Kambô also works very well in combination with sacred plants like Ayahuasca or Iboga. A friend of mine recently came to me who had cancer spreading all over her body. The situation was quite urgent so I started with an intensive protocol of double

treatments twice a week. She had strong trust and an according will power. After a few months, she looked much better. Everybody, including her doctor, was surprised. Indeed, she felt fit, strong and healthy. The results of her blood tests were quite encouraging, and the cancer's growth slowed down.
I noticed, often during her treatments, another personality coming out to the surface. This personality showed herself as a hungry spirit, poor and alone, someone unable to help herself. When this second personality appeared, my patient showed a lot of resistances, complaints and would even get angry with me. On the other hand, she has a very strong personality and fortunately she did not give up on the treatments. Once we explored this 'second personality' together. It came out that it was related to her grandmother whose death was a traumatic experience for her and her family. I told her that whenever that spirit would come back, she might choose to send this spirit away. She then had the awareness to keep calm and breathe when this spirit was tempting her to complain about how poor she was. This experience was a turning point in her healing process with kambô. She had finally chosen to be in her power.
After this, something changed during the treatments. Her process during the kambô treatments became fastened. She lost her resistances and the kambô medicine worked more effective then ever before. In the meantime, her cancer was still growing some, and still threatening her life. After a few months of additional chemo therapy, all traces of the cancer have left and she is fit. This healing process happened in about six months.

Bio-piracy and rights of the Indigenous Tribes
Studies on the indigenous tribes using kambô started in the 1930's. After the 1950's, western scientists became interested in investigating this secretion. In the 1980's, during his visits to the Matses in Peru, anthropologist Peter Gorman documented his experience of the kambô treatment he received. Most of the scientific information you read in this article comes from his article, 'Making Magic.' He sent samples of phyllomedusa bicolor to western universities. In that same time period, pharmaceutical companies registered the first patents of kambô

peptides. Not surprisingly, the global pharmaceutical industry showed a keen interest in the medicinal properties of the frog's secretion as they did in other medicines coming from the Amazon (Notably, the blood pressure medication Captopril was developed in the 1970's from the venom of a Brazilian pit viper). Although some of the peptides found in the frog's secretion have been successfully reproduced in laboratories and patented, it has not led to any new pharmaceuticals being marketed.

In 2003, the Katukinas, guided by chief Fernando, denounced the misuse of kambô and accused the pharmaceutical companies who had patented kambô peptides of bio-piracy. They claimed the rights of the medicine belonged to the Katukinas and other Amazonian tribes. In 2004, an alliance between the Katukinas and the Brazilian government formed, aimed to ensure that profits generated from the development of the kambô's secretion would benefit Brazil. Since then, the Brazilian government has banned the use of kambô in Brazil and any publicity of its properties.

Recently, a new association, M.A.T.S.E.S, has been created in Peru, where kambô is still legal, by Dr. Dan Pantome. The aim of this philanthropic association is to support the native tribes who live in the Amazon and to protect them from speculations made by outsiders. As Dr. Pantone writes, 'protecting the native people of the Amazon means to protect the rainforest' because in this way the rainforest will be not manipulated by the interests of outsiders who don't care about it. The whole area where the Matses live has recently been sold to an international oil company. In the 70's the Matses themselves were bombed by helicopters after they attacked workers who were building a highway on their territory. The cultural changes faced by the indigenous Amazonian tribes are developing at such a fast pace that there is not much time to protect the very developed knowledge their culture has produced. It is good to remind ourselves that an international law to protect these indigenous people, their traditions and the Amazon forest is urgently needed. The knowledge of the indigenous people is a precious gift to mankind, which has already helped many of us. I think we should do everything in our power to protect it.

References
1) P.Gorman, 'Making magic' from Omni, July 1993
2) Marcelo Bolshow Gomes, 'Kambô The Spirit of the Shaman'
3) 'Ruolo dei peptidi antimicrobici nell'immmunita' innata', Universita' di Roma.
Articles and essays
S. A. (1984) Ph.D. dissertation (Columbia University, New York).
V. Erspamer, G. F. & Cei, J. M. (1986) Comp. Biochem. Physiol. C 85, 125-137.
'Sostanze bioattive: dalla pelle di un anfibio al cervello umano', Accademia delle Scienze, Universita' di Roma, La Sapienza, 1987
Copyright © 2016 · Lifestyle Pro Theme on Genesis Framework.

Made in the USA
San Bernardino, CA
27 March 2018